WHAT IF...?

(or Whatever Happened to Common Sense?)

By

MARY FRANCES

ISBN: 978-1-4269-3915-0 (sc)
ISBN: 978-1-4269-3916-7 (hc)
ISBN: 978-1-4269-3917-4 (e)

Library of Congress Control Number: 2010910540

*Our mission is to efficiently provide the world's finest, most comprehensive book publishing
service, enabling every author to experience success. To find out how to publish your book,
your way, and have it available worldwide, visit us online at www.trafford.com*

Trafford rev. 8/09/2010

 www.trafford.com

North America & international
toll-free: 1 888 232 4444 (USA & Canada)
phone: 250 383 6864 ♦ fax: 812 355 4082

To my brother Brian
and the rest of my long-suffering family,
with love.

Also by Mary Frances

Non-fiction
THE SONG OF THE SPINNING SUN

Fiction
ALICE McGINTY'S GOAT

ACKNOWLEDGEMENTS

First of all I particularly wish to thank the philosopher and theologian Keith Ward for his encouragement, for his permission to quote from his book Why there almost certainly is a God, and for his kind and sympathetic comments on WHAT IF...? Many thanks also to Gerard Pomfret of Good News Books for his advice.

My deeply sincere thanks go to Fr Gerry Walsh, and Peter and Mary Rose for their help with Biblical references; to the staff and pupils of Backwell and Gordano schools in North Somerset and to Joseph Meigh and his college friends, all of whom co-operated enthusiastically with my questionnaire, and finally to Nelisile and Thandi Dube, for giving me their own perspectives on today's society.

Most of all, my love and thanks go to my family and friends for their patience and support while it was all coming to fruition – even though some of them did not altogether agree with my arguments (such as they are!)

Without you all, where on earth would I be?

"Help!"

NOT AN APOLOGY

I am not a philosopher. Nor am I a scientist. I have no university degree (Philosophy was not on the curriculum in my 1940s boarding school). In fact, the only pieces of paper I possess that prove I have a brain at all are my Oxford School Certificate (with Matriculation Exemption, I hasten to add), a driving licence and a diploma in journalism - and I'm not at all sure the latter qualifies me for anything other than writing attention-grabbing stories.

My only real assets, of the intellectual kind anyway, are a sense of humour, an overwhelming desire, like Kipling's elephant's child, to know *why* everything, and a common sense approach to problems and arguments which the cleverest people seem to argue and fight over forever and ever amen.

Most of the time, I have to admit, I feel like the small boy in the old Hans Anderson tale of the Emperor's New Clothes. Television, the press and a great many journalists give us their opinions in the firm, decisive sort of way that convinces us they must know best. Character assassinations, partisan political views, world views (you name it) we feel that because "we've seen it on the tv," or "read it in the papers," whatever it is must be right. The greatest victims of this are the poor beleaguered politicians, whom nobody believes any more, no matter what they say or do, and the much-derided subject of religion.

But are the press and television, not to mention one or two philosophers who ought to know better, simply parading their own nakedness in invisible robes which they declare only stupid people can't see?

As you may have guessed by now, WHAT IF...? is born of frustration. It is also the result of 80 years spent rattling around on this beautiful but tormented globe, collecting much colourful experience and many, many bruises.

I am not, therefore, apologising for my views because I am

not trying, and couldn't possibly try, to convince the serious philosophy academics about anything. I wouldn't dare! This book is for the rest of us – the everyday people bewildered by all the arguments raging around them, the Too Tired To Care people, home from work and the school run, frazzled from the supermarket dash for supper, the grappling with homework and tomorrow's lunch boxes - and finally (if they're lucky) the pint or the G & T in front of a late night movie.

If it's any comfort to them or to you, I too have been there, done that and got all possible tee-shirts.

So take heart. Not all intelligentsia can be right at the same time.

CHAPTER ONE

How do we see the world?

It seems to me that what we see depends on where we are when we're looking at it. The view from your upstairs bedroom window will be slightly different from the one on the floor below, and the views from the front and back of the house will be different again.

Take mountains: A geologist will see rock formations and will tell you more or less why and how they came to be there. A climber will be focussing entirely on the next foot-or-handhold and will look on the structure as a challenge. The botanist will be looking for flora, the biologist for fauna, and the family driving past in their people-carrier will see only foothills – useful as a landmark on their journey (or as a possible photo opportunity for bears, if you happen to be in the right country at the right time!) They will see the magnificence, but it won't be their focus.

The children gazing out of the rear window, though, will be looking with different eyes. To them the view will be one of enormity – of majesty and un-thought-of beauty. The mountains will be seen for what they are, whole and entire and awesome.

Do we get so wrapped up in our ways of thinking that we can't see the wood for the trees – or, in this case, the mountain range for the mountains?

Sometimes it takes uncluttered eyes to see life in the round - clear, immense, cruel, mysterious and beautiful.

CHAPTER TWO

"What If...?"

The vast majority of people will admire and respect their awesomely intelligent scientists and philosophers. Many of us will be interested enough to look a bit further. But in the main we just want to get on with our lives, working, shopping, worrying about the kids, playing golf or football, or simply going to the pub for a swift one.

Just as in politics, many people will say (and I quote from experience here). "Why should I bother to vote? Politicians are all the same." So when they ask: "Why bother with religion? What difference does it make?" they are only expressing the same feelings of cynical disillusionment as the rest of us about how things are these days.

With scandal surrounding our politicians, and millennia of wars in the name of religion, who can blame them?

But then again, I suspect it depends on which window we are looking through.

Are we seeing life in the round, or just the bit of it that concerns ourselves?

What if we have missed the point?

CHAPTER THREE

What difference does it <u>really</u> make?

If pressed, most people will admit to wondering "what if...?" now and again.

It starts from early childhood. "What if...there really is a man in the moon?" "What if...Father Christmas really does come down the chimney? How does he get in when we've only got central heating?" "What if...mum and dad don't get home in time to give me my pocket money?" or, of course, "What if...mum and dad don't come home *at all?*"

As we get older the "what ifs" change a bit, but however old we are, all of us at one time or another are going to say "What if...dying is not the end after all?" and "Why are we alive and what's it all for?"

My husband, unlike me, had a string of letters after his name and lived up to them. One day he said: "No-one has ever been truly convinced by an argument, however well put. They may concede a point for now, but as soon as you've gone they will revert to their own opinions."

He may have been right (the jury is still out as far as I am concerned) but if so what can possibly convince us humans? What do the "Yes, buts" and the "Yes, but *surelys*" and the "What ifs?" need to hear or see that is enough to sway their reluctant minds? What are the really big questions of the day that refuse to be solved by learned arguments (often going round and round) and that seem to slide away time after time into the 'not proven' box? "Why are we alive?" and "What is it all for?" are certainly two of the most important ones, but I can think of dozens more.

How are we going to resolve all these questions, bearing in mind that the top brains in the world have always been (and still are) equally divided? If the really clever people can't agree, what chance do we humbler mortals have of working it all out?

So much easier to forget the questions and get on with our lives. Whether or not there is anything after death is something we will find out once and for all anyway, in course of time, no matter what the top brains decide. So why waste time worrying about it now?

Easier said than done, though, isn't it? Despite all our attempts to smother them, the old "What ifs" *will* keep on popping up to disturb our peace.

One of them, though, is the cornerstone, the basic foundation for all the rest. We can go back and back and back, consult geologists, archaeologists, theologists, historians, philosophers and the cleverest scientists – yet no-one, absolutely no-one, has come up with the final definitive answer.

How did it all begin, this wonderful universe?

A good question. Perhaps the only one, if truth be told.

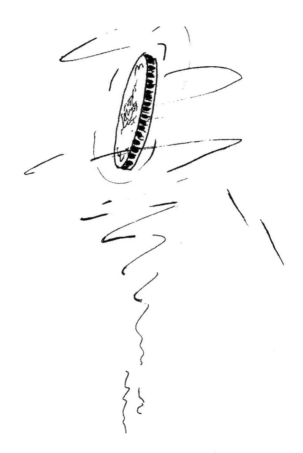

Your call.

CHAPTER FOUR

The Ultimate Gamble

Are you a gambler? If so, what odds do you consider reasonable before they become too much of a risk?

Try this one:

Science and God are not, as you may think (or may have been taught to think) incompatible. The fashion in this country at the moment is to dismiss the God option as superstitious rubbish and leave it at that – but believe it or not, the fact is that in all but one important case the two options actually confirm each other. There is one point, however, where the most eminent scientists, philosophers and theologians are at odds. Was the universe created, or did it come about by an accidental conjunction of forces? And since neither of them can prove conclusively, absolutely and without any doubt whatsoever that their view is right, both sides are left with a 50% chance of being wrong.

Logically, then, the chances are 50/50 for a Creator with a definite purpose in mind, and the possibility of an after-life of some kind – or for existence in an unpredictable world where bad things happen and often do, and with nothing at all at the end of it.   Where will you place your bet?

I have my own preferences, but then I am not you and the decision is always – has to be – yours. You may be accused of hedging your bets, but don't we all do that anyway, all the time? And in this case, the gamble is really and truly a matter of life and death, and whether to hedge or not seems very small beer.

Personal Note: What makes this gamble especially appealing to me personally is that one side always wins hands down, simply by the fact that it cannot lose. For if A spends his time believing in a

Creator with a purpose, and a future other than this one, he will be living in hope and there will be a good, solid meaning to his life. And if he is wrong, it won't matter. Disappointment is impossible, because he won't know!

If, on the other hand, B spends his life believing he is merely an amazing accident of chance and evolution, then existence in an unpredictable, vulnerable world will seem meaningless. One day it will come to a stop with nothing at the end of it. He will have no hope for a future beyond now and whatever can be amassed in the short time available. But if he is wrong he is going to look pretty silly.

Personal Note: Incidentally, I am not the first to consider the question in gambling terms. The French philosopher Blaise Pascal beat me to it by 400 years!

"Belief is a wise wager," he said: "Granted that faith cannot be proved, what harm will come to you if you gamble on its truth and it proves false? If you gain you gain all; if you lose you lose nothing. Wager, then, without hesitation that He exists." (Blaise Pascal – 17th century French philosopher – 1623-1662)

And yes, I know perfectly well that illustrations are not proof, but they are useful all the same (Where would IKEA be without them). I also know that one swallow doesn't make a summer! That doesn't stop it from being beautiful, though, does it?

Personal story: I have always been a fan of the Dick Francis novels – having been secretly in love with his heroes for years – but until last year had never been to any racecourses. So for my birthday a very good friend decided to rectify this by taking me to Chepstow races. It was a beautifully warm, sunny day in May and my day out was perfect from beginning to end.

Not particularly interested in betting myself, being too lost in admiration of the horses being escorted around for our inspection, I had watched my friend consulting his formbook and placing his bets according to what he had learned. He did this several times without winning anything. At the last minute I decided to put a pound on a horse named "Young Jimmy," simply because I knew a ten-year-old boy with that name, and anyway the jockey was a woman.

To my great glee, Young Jimmy romped home in first place, so with my £12 win I treated my friend to tea and cakes at the bar.

I was very amused. Studying statistics may be good but it offers no guarantees, and sometimes an intuitive leap of faith (or blind luck, if you see it that way) works just as well – and now and then even better.

I will certainly never forget that particular Day Out

Incidentally, I never went to another race meeting, so never had a chance to put my theory to the test. So, as all the clever scientists will no doubt point out, this illustration isn't evidence at all.

I know.

(It's fun, though, isn't it?)

CHAPTER FIVE

Here we go round the mulberry bush

Does anyone really enjoy committee meetings? Me, I can't stand them but find myself sitting through them all the same, captive and yawning and trying helplessly to control my drooping eyelids. I do, however, come to life occasionally. A fierce argument breaking out somewhere will do it, or the discussion of something I feel strongly about personally. But what frustrates me most of all is the endless circular debate that seems to tackle everything but the main point.

It's as if saying that $2 + 2 = 4$ is too simple. Let's say instead that two Cox's Orange Pippins, one Granny Smith and a Gala, one of which is cut in half, altogether make five pieces of different kinds of apple $(2 + 2 = 5)$

This is, of course, true - but weren't we supposed to be counting apples, rather than pieces of apple? – a point which has lost itself somewhere in what seems to be an endless debate.

How many of us truly understand whether or not an argument is elegant or whether something is causal or necessary. Does it matter to our everyday lives whether the universe is made of particle dust or cream cheese? Well, of course it *matters* in the long run, but today, here and now, most of us are much more interested in what to have for supper, or which team won yesterday's football match.

And that is why the long, beautifully written volumes that grace our library shelves, written in impeccable prose and batting to and fro rather like intellectual Centre Court matches, very often remain gracing the said shelves while romantic novels, Hello magazine and the sports pages do a better job of holding our attention.

This means, of course, that except for Science or Philosophy students, college lecturers and local study groups, the big questions never get addressed except on over-simplified, highly coloured television documentaries. These are, of course, either taken as bound to be true because they are presented by respected experts, or dismissed as rubbish for exactly the same reason!

Poor chaps, they can't win, can they?

CHAPTER SIX

And/or or Either/or

I am puzzled by the current view in Society at the moment, that Science and Faith are incompatible – enemies, in fact –so that we are left with an either/or choice.

Why?

To me, it seems perfectly logical and reasonable for Science to be simply man's desire to use his considerable, and as yet hardly tapped, intelligence for the purpose of understanding the world and life. Until recently this was beyond our human ability. We just didn't know enough.

Faith in a creator doesn't do away with scientific discovery. Why should it? Why shouldn't a creator *choose* to design us with such astoundingly wonderful and complex brains that we simply have to *find out?* Maybe we have been created to do just that?

Let's say, for example, that a creator caused the Big Bang, and ordered evolution in such a way that extraordinarily intelligent life appeared after aeons of development. Who is to say that he didn't *deliberately* make the intelligent life clever enough to ask questions? Perhaps this creator wants his amazing creation to be valued and admired simply because it is, in fact, amazing. But not just amazing – also beautiful beyond belief, and therefore truly worthy to be valued and admired.

A marvel is not only there to be admired. It is there to be *understood*. And what could be more marvellous than our world of order, beauty and astounding complexity?

True, there are things about it that puzzle and disturb us – pain, for one, and the apparent cruelty of the food chain in action. But more of that later.

CHAPTER SEVEN

Simple or Simplistic?

Because I realise this book will probably be dismissed as *'simplistic'* (when I of course obviously consider my opinions to be *simple* - mere common sense logic), I decided to look those two words up in my Chambers dictionary. This is what it said:

Simple – Consisting of one thing or element, not complex or compound. *(Back to our four apples again?)*.

Simplistic–Tending to over-simplify, making no allowance for the problems and complexities that exist or inevitably arise. (*I am trying – honestly – to be fair and make allowances for all our un-numbered 21st century problems*).

I would therefore add one more Chambers definition:

To complicate– to make complex, to entangle. (*There are enough people doing that already – why add to them?*)

Yes, of course I know life can be, and very often is, exceedingly complicated, but what I find interesting is humankind's tendency to make everything even more complicated than it needs to be.

The real skill, I feel, is recognising the difference.

CHAPTER EIGHT

The Ultimate Firework

The arguments among scientists, philosophers and theologians about the Big Bang have always both puzzled and amused me. Puzzled because so far no-one has come up with a reasonable (well, reasonable to most of us anyway) answer to the question - *who or what lit the blue touch paper?* And amused because it seems there are no hoops many great minds will not put themselves through to prove their point – or simply to disprove a theory they don't personally like! - e.g., if we don't like the world being round, we can always join the Flat Earth Society, or dream up yet another alternative.

We could choose to think of Earth as a CD disc, spinning so fast that it becomes a sort of giant Frisbee. Or perhaps it really is supported by an infinite number of turtles or elephants. (I personally don't believe the earth is a giant Frisbee or supported by elephants because I've been all the way round it on a cruise ship, arriving safely back at my starting point – but of course we are all free to make our own decisions, and maybe I was a victim of hundreds of optical illusions).

Some years ago and probably hidden deep in the BBC archives, there was a series of television documentaries about the Universe given by a scientist/presenter (whose name I have forgotten, if I ever knew it!) which I found suitably fascinating – particularly in the very last programme. In it he said something so astounding that it has remained with me ever since.

He had arrived at the Big Bang point, the very beginning of it all, and told us that after many, many years of research the only conclusion he could possibly come to was that *there had to be a Creator.*

Fine, I thought. At last we have a scientist making a

positive statement one way or the other. But then he went on to say that he didn't like that explanation, so he'd thought of another one – but one which, he was afraid, would take an even greater leap of faith than the first.

My first reaction was: "Why?" Why bother? Why dream up an unbelievably complicated theory full of millions of possible universes simply because you don't like the one you've already described as conclusive?

My second reaction followed hot on the first: He had postulated an endless number of universes with an endless number of possibilities. I had blinked at this. To my inescapably common-sense brain, it doesn't matter how many Big Bangs there were, one or a trillion, trillion, trillions, the question inevitably remains the same. They will all have to have been *started off*. Since they will all be made of perishable matter, they will have a beginning and an end in a ceaseless chicken-and-egg situation. But even chickens and eggs have to have an ultimate beginning, being made of matter as they undoubtedly are. And the more universes there are, the more beginnings there are going to be. Unless, of course, we start with one chicken (or egg?) and one universe, which brings us back to the "who or what started that one off?" question – or we keep our trillions of universes and the question becomes "who or what started *them* off?"

My problem has always been that we have been taught to understand that our solar system exists in a vacuum, and since the only people to venture into this vacuum have been encapsulated in their own safe little cabins, we have no evidence to show us otherwise. I have also been told that since nothing ever exists in a vacuum, there can be no forces, no elements, in fact nothing to make a bang *with* whether big or little. And if by chance I learn that the vacuum in our universe is not a vacuum at all, but full of its own kind of *stuff*, the question still remains.

How did it get there?

Personal Note: If there can be limitless space and limitless universes, why can there not be a limitless mind?

And no matter how intelligent we are, we have never succeeded in actually creating life. We can only clone it. As any yogurt maker will know, one needs a morsel of live material, a living organism, to start things off.

CHAPTER NINE

So what are the alternatives?

All matter has a beginning and an end. It gets born and eventually dies. If everything made of matter came into being (without other matter starting it off) there must be something or someone existing *outside* it. Something or someone that is *non-matter.*

If this *non-matter* is powerful enough to have thought up and created a vast universe like ours, then it must be very powerful indeed. Powerful enough to stop everything it has begun, if it chose.

The earth turns completely on its axis every 24 hours – that is, at approximately 1,000 miles per hour (close to the equator – less if nearer the two Poles). And there we were, thinking 120mph in a Ferrari was eye-crossingly fast. Imagine that speed multiplied by nine or ten with ourselves standing upright in the middle of it and your eyes will indeed cross with disbelief.

I happened to be sitting in my garden one perfect summer evening, gazing up into a breathtakingly blue sky with painted-on wisps of white fleece. A pigeon stared at me from the rooftop, and behind me a grey squirrel was investigating a cylinder of nuts hanging from the cherry tree. And I realized with awe that all of us – pigeon, squirrel, the cherry tree and me – were whirling at undreamt of and totally unbelievable speed. (Not only 1,000 mph on its own axis, but revolving at a staggering one million miles per day around the sun in an outer spiral arm of the galaxy! Woweee!)

Why does the world seem so still when we are really whizzing faster than any of us can contemplate? Can it really be true? If it is, what would happen to us if it suddenly whirled even faster - or stopped whirling altogether?

Since what hold us firmly to the earth are centrifugal force and the weight of the atmosphere, the result would be a bit spectacular. We would all drop off – except that the earth would certainly break up or burn up first, which I am reliably informed would be the case.

Obviously no-one in his right mind wants this to happen, yet there is absolutely nothing we can do about it. If we believe we are accidents then all we can do is hope an asteroid doesn't halt us in our frenetic tracks. But if we decide there is an all-powerful creator, we have also to decide what kind of creator he/she/it could possibly be, and what he/she/it would be likely to do about this whirling, spinning business.

There is quite a lot of choice here.

CHAPTER TEN

What kind of creator?

There seems, at first glance, to be plenty of creator-type beings to choose from. There are the Greek gods (and heaven knows there are enough of those!). We can think of something or someone who made the universe in a spare moment, then grew bored and forgot about it. There is even a creator who made it for fun and has been having fun with it (and us) ever since. We can even invent names – The Universe, Energy, the Fates are just three out of many. (I am discounting the idea of aliens from another galaxy, because aliens too would have had to be created in their turn). Just to make it even stranger than it is already, I've heard people say "The Universe is friendly," and "If the Fates allow," which pre-supposes some sort of outside control even by the very people who say there is no God. Or are the friendly universe and the generous fates just more coincidences to add to the millions we come across every day?

In our present culture we have different gods altogether, the strictly earthly ones of power and money and fame, youth and beauty, all of which come to an abrupt end when we die so are out of the running for the role of Creator.

All the major religions, however, agree on one thing – that there was/is in fact a creator of some kind. They may have different names for this Power or see it from a different perspective, but they have all come down firmly on the God theory rather than the accidental one.

But if we are looking at evidence (which I am trying to do to the best of my limited ability) we have to admit there is precious little to back up any of the "Universe", "Energy" or "adolescent, mischievous God" options. 'The Universe' is made of matter just like us. 'Energy' alone is not enough. It must have a source, which of course could be inspired by an Eternal mind but which otherwise could not exist by itself. For now it can only be seen or felt by its results – i.e. lightning, bedside lamps and dishwashers. The Fates merely suggests an unidentified outside source giving us no control over our circumstances.

Philosophies, ideas, visions, even personal preferences – these we have in their hundreds. But evidence?

Right!

How about the many thousands of years of written history, in many forms but always reporting the same basic facts? According to those, there is one Creator whose existence has been recorded over aeons of time, on tablets of stone, on papyrus, then on printed paper, in the form of letters, personal accounts of events many thousands of years ago. He has even been recorded in our own past history.

This creator we call God, but only because the name he used for himself in answer to Moses' question was "I AM" (Exodus 3 v 14 and John 8: 58) which isn't in our culture and doesn't make sense to us. It does rather indicate, though, that someone who is "I AM" might just be eternal!

This God, however, left some useful guidelines for our survival – written on those tablets of stone (hard to destroy in our shredders). And the astonishing thing about these instructions is that they are still being used to this day as the basis of our legal system. Not only are our own UK laws built on them, the laws of most of Western civilization are too.

So instead of looking around for an adolescent, mischievous creator, or a bored, uninterested one, I am listing the rules laid down for us by the only god for whom we have any kind of evidence, either written or personal.

These can all be found in any Bible, in the Book of Deuteronomy (chapter 5 verses 6-21)

It should be noted that these instructions are not spoil-sport do's and don'ts but guidelines for not injuring, maiming or otherwise destroying ourselves and/or other people. They are for our benefit.

Or are they? How can we be sure?

The fairest way to find out, one way or another, is to consider them with an open mind. In short - Creator or no Creator, what happens if we ignore them?

CHAPTER ELEVEN

The D I Y manual

Are you a handy DIY person? Are you good at putting together self-assembly furniture? Me, I have to admit that whatever I assemble promptly disassembles itself in short order – and I have a four-legged table with three legs, a collapsed stool and numerous small and now useless items to prove it. If you are female and even remotely like myself, the chances are that you will read the instructions, follow them to the letter, and then, after many rude words, give up!

If you are male, however, you may well try your hand at putting whatever-it-is together without recourse to the instructions at all. You are a man, aren't you? and men are supposed to be good at that sort of thing. Until, that is, you find yourself with sundry spare parts which seem to have no place anywhere, or discover (to your secret embarrassment) that you have assembled Part A where Part C should have been and whatever-it-is is now upside down.

But how about these instructions for life which have been written into the laws of our land? What exactly are they?

Actually, the Bible calls them the Ten Commandments, and they've been part of our rules of conduct since records began. Unfashionable and inconvenient they may be, but they also make a great deal of sense – once we have overcome our national dislike of religious-type words! We just have to ignore the wording and get down to basics!

Personally, I prefer to think of them as our D I Y Rules. That is, after all, what they are when all's said and done. (Traditionalists, please forgive me for paraphrasing the Commandments of God. I really don't think he will mind, and anyway I am not the first!)

The First D I Y Rule - I am your God. Do not have any others.

The Second – Do not take the name of the Lord your God in vain.

The Third - Remember to keep My day holy.

The Fourth - Honour your father and mother

The Fifth – Do not kill

The Sixth – Do not commit adultery

The Seventh –Do not steal

The Eighth - Do not bear false witness against your neighbour.

Ninth – Do not covet your neighbour's wife

The Tenth – Do not covet your neighbour's goods.

The Jewish law and the Orthodox and Eastern Christian churches are based on exactly the same principles, except for a couple of variations in where they appear in the list. And since the Commandments are the foundation of our justice system it's worth taking a look at what happens when they are broken.

They were, after all, given as principles of moral behaviour for the human race. Ignoring them may not be such a good idea.

CHAPTER TWELVE

The First D I Y Rule -
I am your God. Do not have any others.

This is an easy one. If we don't believe in a Creator God, what is to stop us from worshipping who and where we like, or using his name as a swearword whenever we feel like it?

Strange gods can leave us with some strange problems.

As for the rest of the ten, do they really work? Do they really stop us from playing with matches or running into the middle of a busy road without looking? Or are we only concerned with the 11th commandment that says: "Thou shalt not be found out."

There are of course un-numbered non-believers who live wonderfully good lives - not for any hope of a future heaven but because they feel it is the only just way to live. (I was one those once, so completely understand this point of view). They do their best not to harm others but to help them - giving time and energy to voluntary work and donating generously to Children In Need, as well as to hundreds of charities less well publicised. What's more, they do it all out of a sense of fair play, with no thought of any eternal reward.

What happens to this sense of fair play, though, when powerful emotions like jealousy, anger or revenge take us by the throat? Is the motivation of being a "good person" enough then? I can't answer for the rest of mankind, but can say for myself, without hesitation, that *no it isn't*.

Making gods of material things, however, is another matter again, and comes into play when some things become so indispensable that they must be put on their shiny pedestals and worshipped.

We all know those gods exist, and we all run the risk of

being seduced by them – if we fail to see the warning signs in time.

So what are these strange gods that we're tempted into worshipping? And what are the results if we do?

Personal Note: "What has God ever done for me?" is a familiar reason for not believing in a creator. The same people tend to take all the credit for things going right but blame God for everything that goes wrong. (Hardly fair, I would have thought. After all, one can't have it both ways.)

Two lovely examples in my own life are when my husband lost his wallet and rang me in desperation. When he rang again ten minutes later, knowing quite well that I would have been asking God to find it for him, he said: "Don't go giving God the credit - I suddenly remembered where to look."

The other example is when a friend sent me an urgent letter. She needed a quick prayer for a seemingly insoluble problem. Weeks later I rang to ask what had happened. Her reply was "Oh it all worked itself out beautifully. I needn't have bothered you."

On a final note, parents who teach their children nothing about God but everything about Science (on the premise that the children can make up their own minds when they are older) – are, in my personal opinion, depriving them of the power of choice. How can one make comparisons knowing only one side of an argument? It would be like spinning a double-headed coin and asking children to call heads or tails, or asking them if they prefer carrots to broccoli when you have never given them broccoli.

CHAPTER THIRTEEN

Just a few of our 21ˢᵗ century gods

1 - The Science god

This is definitely the fashionable God, the one a great many people seem to subscribe to (and worship, come to that), particularly in our Western culture. But what exactly does it mean?

According to a questionnaire sent to two senior schools in North Somerset, the answer seems to be the same old one we've dealt with already – If there's no creator, the universe must have come about by accident, starting with the Big Bang. So there is nothing to worship but a cold series of sums and formulae signifying a cold, dark empty space.

And what can this empty space do for us?

Well, we can fill it with electronic gadgets, nice houses, holidays and gardens with swimming pools, but in the end we just go back to where we came from – dust!

Personal Note: Who was it said: "Without hope a society dies"? George Orwell's book "1984" describes in clear detail what does happen in a hopeless society..

21ˢᵗ century god 2 - The Money god

Let's face it, the Money god isn't exactly trustworthy, is it? Funds have a way of suddenly disappearing. All we need is a recession, a bank disaster or sudden redundancy and there we are, bankrupted and very likely on the streets.

Even when we have it, it never seems to be enough. New Ipods are suddenly updated, mobile phones become trickier and cleverer and our spring wardrobe is out of date by autumn. Even our five-bedroomed houses are suddenly not big enough. Country views and swimming pools become "must haves" overnight.

We also run the risk of growing into misers, which is far from funny. Eaten up with the fear of being poor, we can tuck away our millions in secret bank accounts or hide them under the bed and live in squalor and misery.

Unfortunately we do actually need the stuff. Without money we starve or die of exposure. It only becomes a problem when the lust for it turns into obsession and we ruin relationships, develop ulcers and die of stress at 45!

And anyway we *can't take it with us.*

Personal Note: Of course there are huge advantages to being super-rich. One only has to watch tv programmes like "The Secret Millionaire," or read of private wealth sent quietly to countries in desperate poverty, to know that Money can and does work wonderful and remarkable miracles. Unfortunately this is not always the case. I was once on a cruise ship with elderly women who joined the same ship year after year. Since they spent their time complaining bitterly about what they thought of as the deterioration of the service, I asked three of them why they chose to keep coming if they weren't enjoying themselves. Their answer? "What else is there to do with the money?"

I was shocked, and could have suggested a million ways of spending their extra cash (e.g. giving it to landmine victims, endowing orphanages, even passing a bit of it on to me), but desisted because they would have been scandalised in their turn and anyway it wouldn't have made any difference. .

21ˢᵗ century god 3 -
The Youth and Beauty god

Youth and Beauty have now taken on Goddess status. How many otherwise perfectly sane women have spent massive amounts of money on nips, tucks, injections and major surgery, turning themselves into Queen Canutes and ordering the tide of age to ripple obediently backwards? Not to mention the teenage girls who have starved themselves close to death – if not to death itself – because they long to be tall and skinny fashion models, or like the latest singing phenomenon whispering into, and apparently eating, her microphone?

Then there is the ceaseless barrage of hair colour and shampoo adverts, where the first hint of grey is treated with horror, and where line-ups of beautiful girls bounce their way across our screens, swinging gloriously long, wonderfully thick and richly coloured locks from side to side?

As for the slinky models, one trip to a photographic studio can teach us how to trim our widening torsos with one flick of a computer mouse.

Let's face it, one simply *isn't cool* unless one is slim and young and beautiful – which is hard luck because so few of us are - and even the young grow old in the end.

Personal note: To be fair, I use branded skin care myself, but then I am old enough to have sprouted the lines and wrinkles. And as for hair colour, my chestnut brown locks turned white before the age of 30, so I spent a third of a lifetime dyeing (and ultimately ruining) the hair I was born with.

I did eventually lose the battle while, astonishingly, winning the war. The hair colour I found underneath all the dyeing and rinsing suited me far better than the ones I had been spending my money and time on.

Better still, the new colour matched the new skin tones that were changing with age, so I saved on cosmetics too. And finally, too many tucks can spoil your smile. Worshipping the god of youth and beauty takes its toll.

21ˢᵗ century god 4 - The Sex god

This particular god appears to have become the norm. Television soaps, plays and documentaries take it for granted. No book is easily publishable without its quota of explicitly described Goings On. In fact, it has become so established as everyday behaviour that we can feel unused, unwanted and downright failures if we are not 'getting any.'

I have decided that, despite all its protestations, media hype *creates* trends, rather than merely following them. And teenagers, subject to their daily fixes of television, and magazines showing their heroes and heroines having their goings-on gloriously broadcast to the world, all naturally rush to join in.

At what cost?

Teenage pregnancies? (I don't know the latest statistics but suspect they would be out of date even before I could quote them). Children have the right to be children while they still have the chance. Being grown up lasts a painfully long time.

Transmittable diseases? These are now accepted with aplomb. "Don't worry too much if you get a dose of something, because your doctor, or the hospital, will give you something to take it away." Except for AIDS, of course, when aplomb isn't going to help you much.

Unwanted babies? Well, they can be dispensed with, can't they? Abortion is treated as a way of life (or death!)

How about internet-fostered paedophilia? Or any other kind of paedophilia for that matter? When young children are so aware of sex, it is hardly surprising that older sex addicts take advantage of all the lovely, fresh fertile soil being prepared for them by non-stop media coverage?

Finally, there are the victims who grow up in a promiscuous

culture where recreational sex is something one does at the weekend after clubbing.

To quote a friend: "When they meet someone really special, what will the girls have left to do to show their partners they *are* special?"

What indeed?

And when the hyped sex eventually becomes boring (for after all there are only so many ways of enjoying it - even the Kama Sutra runs out of ideas in the end) what throne will we find to worship at next?

Personal Note: A few years ago I watched a small boy being interviewed on television. One of the questions was: "What is love?" His reply? "When two people go to bed together."

Excuse me? How about the love of parent, child, friends and family? Country?

From someone or somewhere that small boy had learned that sex is all *there is.*

21ˢᵗ century god 5 - The Fame god

Most of us have watched the X Factor, or Britain's Got Talent at some point. The tears and the despair, the dramas and the elation when they do or don't pass to the next stage are almost unbearable to watch. "This is my dream," they say, as they put themselves through intolerable stress and (all too often) humiliation in front of millions of viewers - the Dream Come True held like a carrot before their star-struck noses.

The fact that all these unnervingly stressful live soaps make wonderful viewing tells us what voyeurs we all are. These are mostly young, vulnerable minds going through hell before our eyes.

Why do they do it?

They do it because Fame is now a household god. The

press and television worship it – and why not? It has turned itself into the money-spinner of all time.

But have we asked ourselves what happens afterwards? How do the winners fare once they have achieved this wonderful zenith, the mountain-top, the being recognised and asked for autographs – plus of course the possibility of "Dream Come True" wealth?

Unfortunately, fame rarely lasts. The public, as well as the press, love playing the let's-build-her-up-and-then-knock-her-down game. How many times do we see heroes and heroines raised on their shiny, sequinned pedestals, only to have their private lives violated, their marriages wrecked or their health ruined by alcohol or mind-changing drugs?

A very lucky few survive, mostly by keeping themselves and their families detached from the press. For the rest of us, this wonderful fame is followed by the terrible, never-ending stress of trying to keep it. How many of our Celebs are on their third or fourth marriages? And how many more are hospitalised for addiction, or hauled before a judge for possession?

And what about the losers? What becomes of them? We are never told.

Finally, get too used to fame and one starts to believe one's own publicity. Never a good idea. Our once adoring fans have a way of tearing us off our plinths.

Personal note: There are, of course, real advantages to fame. Celebrities are given the chance to raise vast sums for charities. A gala function organised by unknown Me might raise a few hundred pounds. The same event organised by the latest idol would result in many thousands, possibly millions of pounds.(viz: Children In Need, the Tear Fund, Childline....).

But apart from the money angle, ordinary people wedged into their particular comfort zones can be stimulated into leaving them – to reach for higher goals, to aim for the summit. An advantage indeed. That is, until the fame grows misty and disappears from public consciousness. Or the new idol succumbs to the old, old lures.

Unfortunately, the lured victims don't have to be young. I was at school with the wife of an actor who achieved fame overnight. The wife and I remained friends, so I saw at first hand the astonishing change this overnight fame caused. Her husband went from jovial, cheerful and hospitable to suspicious, arrogant and downright rude in an amazingly short space of time. He rarely reverted to his jovial, kindly persona, which was rather unfortunate for all concerned.

He was not alone in this experience. I have personally known many others, and will no doubt stumble upon more as time goes by.

I hope not, but then for people like me Hope Springs Eternal.

21ˢᵗ century god 6 – The Power god

Of all the gods, the Power god must be the most pernicious. It affects all the rest. The yachts and the BMWs are only outward signs of the power money gives us. Rape is well known to be more about power than lust. We all know the adage "Power corrupts", well there is another even more potent. "The greater the power the more dangerous the abuse" (Edmund Burke 1729-1797)

Think 'Hitler'!

Luckily, the dictators who believe they rule the world do eventually get their come-uppence. The adage "What goes around comes around" is particularly true in this case. Be nasty and arrogant towards enough people and they will eventually be nasty and arrogant towards you. The trouble is that the despots can do so much damage before being unseated that it's too late for their victims - history can be changed and millions can die in the process.

The Power god, then, is the most dangerous of all. It encourages tiny, antlike creatures to believe they can totally dominate not only their own lives but everyone else's, not to mention the natural world and even the universe itself.

The solitary ant on my garden path might just as easily try to dominate me.

Personal Note: According to the Bible, lusting for power was man's undoing. The Adam and Eve story (Genesis 3: v-6) may or may not be factually true, but the principle remains the same. They were told they could eat anything except the fruit of one tree. Then a rotten old serpent suggested that if they did they would become like God himself. So they took a fateful bite.

Alas, it didn't work.

Alas it never does.

CHAPTER FOURTEEN

The Second D I Y Rule - Swearwords

What can one possibly say about the second DIY rule – not taking God's name in vain – except that it has well and truly gone through the window.

How about *"Oh – My – Gaaaaard!"* in astonishment, or simply *"Oh God!"* in irritation or frustration. Then there is *"Jesus Christ."* An everyday expression of rage or shock.

Why? The F word is used enough, often cropping up at least three times in every sentence like a sort of alternative comma. So why use a sacred one?

Maybe it's because it *is* sacred. 'Anything Goes' applies to Western culture as much as it has ever done, if not more. Whatever is sacred to someone will be fair game to someone else, except of course in some countries, where using the name of God in vain may well have unfortunate results. Definitely not a good idea. (Remember Salman Rushdie, pursued by a Fatwa for his *Satanic Verses*?).

But what happens to us if we disobey this instruction? Not a lot in terms of material existence. The sky doesn't fall on us, nor do we get hit by lightning. True, it upsets other people and limits our vocabulary, but if there is no God what does it matter anyway?

But what if there is?

Personal Note: In the novel ALICE McGINTY'S GOAT, the heroine has great fun making up swearwords. Anything with nice, positive consonants and vowel sounds is used in moments of exasperation, doubt or despair. And all of them can be quoted with impunity! Try that one, too. It's fun, and a good test of creativity.

CHAPTER FIFTEEN

The Third D I Y Rule –
Sunday, Day of Rest?

Here's another "D I Y rule" that has definitely bitten the dust. Society assumes that "no-one goes to church on Sunday any more". Why should they, when there is no God, so no reason for churches at all? Besides, it's *so* un-cool!

Well, it may be un-cool but it has to be said Christianity itself – in all its different denominations and in different parts of the world - seems to be doing very nicely thank you. It just seems impossible to kill it off.

According to Adherents.com, 85% of the American population is considered to be Christian, and there are parts of Africa and South America where Christianity makes up more than 80% of the total population. In Brazil it is 95%!.

Some churches are growing apace, with a large proportion of teenagers and massive family congregations. These are mostly Pentecostal and Evangelical, but the Baptists and (yes!) the Roman Catholics are quietly proliferating – although the press and television seem to dislike reporting them! Huge public events are often treated as though they hadn't happened at all.

"Ignore them and they'll go away" seems to be the general policy.

I, of course, admit to doing my own wandering through supermarkets later in the day, or engaging in laundry which can't be done during the week – so am I being hypocritical? I think not. I do those things *after* going to church, and then I set out to enjoy a free day – freedom in this case being 'doing what I like doing' (which may or may not include wandering through supermarkets or stuffing clothes into automatic washing machines!)

What happens if we ignore our Day Off? The world doesn't come to a shattering end, but Sunday is supposed to be a day of recovery after the week's stresses, so if we find ourselves working in shops and supermarkets while the lucky 'day-off' customers can have a lie-in and do their own shopping – well, we can be forgiven for feeling aggrieved.

Even the Creator had his day off. (Genesis 2 v 3).

CHAPTER SIXTEEN

The Fourth D I Y Rule -
Honouring mum and dad.

What can one possibly say about this in our 21st century culture? The rule of the child is now practically absolute. There are scarcely any sanctions. Disgruntled children, thwarted of the thing they want *right now,* can always win by using Violet Elizabeth's tactic in Richmal Crompton's *Just William* books. She thcreamed and thcreamed until she was thick.

Violet Elizabeth always got her way, but at least it wasn't in her power (as it is in our present culture) to accuse a parent or teacher of abuse and *get away with it?*

If we have no bottom-line moral laws to work with, what are we left with? "Every man for himself?" "Look after Number One because no-one else will?" "I have a right to be happy, so everyone else can whistle?"

Has anyone but me ever wondered why it doesn't seem possible to teach discipline here at home in the UK? Or when this descent into near teenage anarchy really began? (My apologies to Supernanny, who has indeed shown us a way).

Of course they have, but since Society has thrown the babies Faith and Respect out with the bathwater, the only doll they can find to put in their place is materialism. And materialism breeds *disrespect.* It leads to selfishness, and selfishness leads to anarchy. Hence our youthful monsters.

Personal Note: A few years ago, there was a news item on the radio – a leading psychologist had suggested that belief in Santa Clause should be fostered because children need a father figure – someone to look up to.

Ho Hum!.

I am not, of course, suggesting that Santa should be killed off. He's part of the fun of Christmas, as I well know. It was merely the suggestion that he was the only benevolent father figure that struck me as bizarre. God is dead, long live Father Christmas.

CHAPTER SEVENTEEN

The Fifth D I Rule –
No Killing

This is an easy one. Well, easy in theory, in view of the legal system and of how many of us watch Midsomer Murders, and Taggart and repeats of Morse, but not so simple in practice – especially when our young men are taught to kill as a matter of routine.

But murder itself?

Simple, my dear Watson. If we're caught, we go to prison, probably for a very long time. If we're not caught, we spend the rest of our lives in the fear of being caught, especially now with clever tools like DNA. Or with guilt hangovers and more violence, making it even more likely that we really *will* be caught.

There are, of course, some legitimate reasons for killing - i.e. If someone came for my children with an axe I would certainly hit him/her with the nearest weighty object. But although self defence – or defence of one's country – is excusable it is always, *always* regrettable.

The 5th D I Y rule is probably the only one with which Society agrees, whatever it believes.

Just as well, I would have thought!

CHAPTER EIGHTEEN

The Sixth D I Y Rule -
Alas, Adultery is OUT

Ah now, here's the rub! In our present society, promiscuity is very nearly the norm. And adultery is now called "cheating" or "playing away" and more or less taken for granted.

In theory, that is. In practice, as we all know, infidelity costs – and the price is high.

First of all, divorce is expensive. Legal costs, house sales, removals and settlements all use up a great deal of money.

Secondly, it destroys trust, even where it doesn't end in divorce.

Thirdly, there are bereaved, problem children to be pacified.

We have to admit, though, that the best of us will be tempted from time to time, turning a conveniently blind eye to the fact that the consequences are invariably dire.

We can even stop caring. After all, "what partners don't know won't hurt them." Unfortunately this only holds good until the partner finds out. Then it's pay-back time.

Joking apart, the wounds can take a long time to heal.

Personal Note: Once again, I know parents of split families who have somehow survived most of their past traumas and have brought up well behaved young persons with hopeful futures, (at least they are always well behaved in my presence. What they do when I'm not there is something I am never likely to find out).

A story: An elderly couple hobbled into a solicitor's office saying they wanted a divorce. The astonished solicitor asked them why they had waited so long before deciding to separate.

"Well," the wife said, "you see, we had to wait until the children died!"

CHAPTER NINETEEN

The Seventh D I Y Rule -
No stealing

Apart from professional burglars, we will all agree with this one – except of course when it comes to the office paper-clips or phone calls at the firm's expense - or successfully evaded income tax.

The law comes down forcefully on thieves but somehow or other never seems to stop them – possibly because the profit from stealing is worth the years or so we spend in gaol? Or is it because a great many thefts are caused by addicts desperately trying to pay for their next fix?

Whatever the motivation for pinching someone else's things, it has always been with us. In Victorian times culprits were either hung or dispatched forthwith to Australia, squashed for months into holds of sailing ships with diseases and cockroaches and often brutal attendants.

In some countries, thieves can still have their fingers or hands chopped off. What an appalling thought! Personally, I am extremely relieved our system of government doesn't go in for lopping bits off me.

Of course, if we are accidents of nature, we will only respect other peoples' property if their need is greater than ours. If we want it more than they do our perspective changes abruptly. "Every-man-for-himself' obviously applies here too. "You've got two and I haven't got any, so I'm going to take one of yours!"

Personal Note: It has often occurred to me to wonder what burglars do when someone burgles them.

CHAPTER TWENTY

The Eighth D I Rule –
Don't tell malicious tales.
(i.e. bear false witness)

Not long ago I qualified as a journalist and spent six or so very happy years writing for our local newspaper. 20 years before that I had been a politician, serving on our City Council as a ward representative. Both those experiences have taught me, as nothing else could have done, how easy it is to bear false witness against just about anybody – and for just about any reason (but mostly in order to achieve a good story)

As a politician I suffered from misreporting, misquoting and politely worded abuse – well, some of it was polite! As a journalist I tried not to fall into any of those traps, but realised quite clearly how easy it is to change the whole meaning of a quotation by putting the words in a different order - or leaving words out – or simply quoting something that the poor victim hasn't even said. To pick out just one sentence can alter the meaning of an entire speech.

That, of course, is how newspapers and magazines make their money, not to mention some political spin-doctors who use it for even more reprehensible reasons. We are not motivated in the same way in our everyday lives.

Or are we?

How about the itty-bitty gossip we all indulge in from time to time? And the 'No smoke without fire' maxim which is insidious, starting rumours on no grounds at all, thereby coating completely innocent victims in undeserved grime.

'Bearing false witness' simply means passing on disagreeable truths (or lies) about someone else, and there are as many ways of doing it as there are people walking the earth. The temptation to feel bigger by making someone else seem smaller can be irresistible.

Unfortunately for us, the person on the receiving end may well retaliate and give us back more than we bargained for.

CHAPTER TWENTY-ONE

The Ninth D I Y Rule -
Coveting the neighbour's wife

The difference between this and Adultery is simple – Adultery is just doing what so far we've only fantasised about. Fancying our next-door neighbour paves the way nicely for positive action.

Appreciation of beauty is one thing, lusting after it can be like taking home a wild tiger and trying to tame it.

A dangerous pastime.

The tooth and claws will get you in the end.

CHAPTER TWENTY-TWO

The Tenth D I Y Rule -
Coveting the neighbour's goods

We seem to be back at stealing again, only, like adultery and coveting, this one means lusting after our best friend's MP3 player. It includes uncomfortable things like envy and jealousy. Why should Mr A live in a mansion with a swimming pool and tennis courts, when I'm in an upstairs flat with no lift? What has he done to deserve it – except perhaps learn to kick a football into a net – or murmur breathily into a microphone?

And why should Mrs A swan around in designer clothes just because she is married to Mr A (or divorced from him with massive alimony)?

We all know the feeling, (me too). In one way or another, we have all been there. So what's the problem? Our private thoughts aren't hurting anyone, are they?

The problem is that envy makes us dissatisfied with what we have. It can, of course, spur us on to greater things, but mostly it takes us on to jealousy, resentment and bitterness, and all three can ruin our lives.

Jealousy alone is a fire that consumes and destroys. It must be one of the most destructive emotions known to homo sapiens.

The other is fear.

CHAPTER TWENTY-THREE

Fear and Jealousy

In 1933 Franklin D Roosevelt said: "Let me assert my firm belief that the only thing we have to fear is fear itself"

He was right, of course. My father lay wounded in a trench in the First World War, half buried under two dead bodies, while the enemy aimed shells directly at his trench every few seconds, without ceasing, for almost 24 hours. He died many thousands of deaths in the fear and certainty that the next shell would be his last. The fact that the two dead bodies were blown off him, leaving him untouched, must have left him with trauma too hard to describe. I have read the story of that day, and can even now feel his terror as a tangible force.

What it also left him with was an eternal gratitude and appreciation for being alive, despite a stiff leg and wounds that had to be dressed every day until he died. He fathered seven children, none of whom would have existed if he had died in that trench. The last of the seven was me, and because I was born on the very anniversary of that day in 1915, I like to think I was special. A sort of talisman?

We all know fear. It has an intense, destructive power and even gives off its own particular scent. Most of us (well, I do anyway) envy the apparently fearless people who scale mountains, do death-defying ski jumps or dig themselves tunnels and vanish into them, not to mention sky-divers and bunji-jumpers - and, maddest of all – entertainers who swallow fire or stop bullets with their teeth!

I don't really suppose these heroes are without any fear at all. Presumably they just thrive on the adrenaline rush that comes with it.

Well done them, I say, but please leave me out. I can survive quite happily without that kind of motivation.

Truly, though, fear is the mainspring of most violence. Fear of being the underdog, fear of losing face, or losing land, or losing oil fields.

Fear can galvanise normally sane, kindly people into doing insane, outrageous things – fear of people whose skin is a different colour, fear of danger to our children from paedophiles, fear of strangers bursting into our homes at night, and fear of domination by other political parties or countries.

Alas, there's nothing new about lynching.

Was it fear of 'difference' that sent Hitler into his orgy of killing? Is it the fear of being usurped that leads all dictators to violently rid themselves of anyone who disagrees with them?

If we really are accidents in time and space, what's to stop us from behaving in the same way? Do we have inbuilt moral standards which forbid such extremes (and if so, where did they come from?) – or do we individually simply not have the power?

An uncomfortable question.

As for Jealousy, that seems to be the dark underbelly of love mixed up somewhere or other with fear of loss. We are jealous when love becomes need and we are faced with the possibility of losing, or never having, what we want so badly – a spouse or partner being enticed away from us by someone else – a promotion given to a colleague who doesn't deserve it – the house of our dreams being snatched away by a purchaser with cash in hand.

I suppose, put simply, fear is the worry of something bad happening. Jealousy is blaming someone else when the bad thing actually happens.

Both fear and jealousy can eat us up.

Personal Note: For God believers there is the comforting thought that Jesus' first words were often either "Fear not" or "Peace be with you."

CHAPTER TWENTY-FOUR

Revenge

Anyone who has ever watched a Laurel and Hardy film will understand why Getting Our Own Back is a dangerous game. You just never know where it's going to stop. Fun to start with, maybe, but oh, dearie me, how swiftly it can descend into mayhem and chaos.

Scenario: Jack feels annoyed enough with Bill to take a pair of scissors and cut off Bill's tie, whereupon Bill retaliates by filling Jack's hat with something horribly sludgy, then pressing it firmly on Jack's head. Things then slide rapidly downhill until they are left with a broken bicycle, a burnt out car, two houses with smashed windows and one chimney fire.

In the end, of course, neither of them has won and both are left with ruined property and a huge repair bill – if not arrest for wilful damage and a hauling before the nearest magistrate (possibly the nearest gaol?)

Of course we know the old Laurel & Hardy films were funny. They always made me laugh and were obviously meant merely as entertainment – but the same principle applies anyway to all of us.

Think "Vendetta".

Think Northern Ireland.

Think Israel.

Personal Note: Much safer solutions are tolerance and not bearing grudges. In short, forgiveness! Hard to do, yes, but "A soft answer turneth away wrath but grievous words stir up anger," (Proverbs 15:1). And anyway, life is too short…!

CHAPTER TWENTY-FIVE

What it boils down to

The problem with the "No Creator, No Ultimate Purpose" option, is that we don't have any rules except the civilised ones of kindness and good manners - which only work if enough people choose to keep them. Even the laws of the land (whichever one we happen to be living in) can't be trusted because they can change according to who is in power at the time.

After that, there is very little more to be said. We seem to be left with "Every man for himself" – or "Choose your god today. You can always change it tomorrow!"

There are, of course, many other gods to be adored, and some of them are very strange indeed, but if I were to specify and enlarge on them all I would probably have to write ten more books.

Meanwhile, I have to admit that throwing out the rulebook doesn't work very well. Like disobeying dad when he tells us not to play with matches, breaking rules might seem like fun at the time but the results can be extremely painful – not to say terminal.

So what about this Creator option? What are the consequences on our everyday lives of actually believing in him/her/it? For who is really interested in anything *but* living their everyday lives? (apart from scientists and philosophers whose 'satiable curiosity is, like mine, the spur to *finding out?*)

CHAPTER TWENTY-SIX

A Frightening Idea?

Many people – especially us reserved Brits – bristle and wriggle away from any talk that looks as if it may have God or Religion in it. It's as though we are being asked embarrassing questions about our personal habits.

Why? What is so frightening about the idea of God? Is it because, in our country in this enlightened century, believing in him is unfashionable? Un-cool? Is it because we are afraid of being laughed at, derided, "put down" as victims of an out-dated superstition? Or worse still, called dupes and labelled "insane"?

Or is it because they think of God as a white-haired old headmaster in the sky, wagging an admonitory finger at us and telling us off for not doing our homework – a stern figure who vents his wrath by sending us hurricanes and earthquakes and killing off innocent children in tsunamis and endless wars?

Perhaps they are simply afraid that believing in a God – any God – will involve them in some sort of commitment or responsibility?

Eeek! "Commitment?" "Responsibility?" What dirty words they have turned out to be? We all know our rights, but how many of us know or care about other peoples', or what we are personally expected to give in our turn? As for God, if he is the spoil-sport who gives us a lot of do's and don'ts, and stops us having any fun, why *should* we talk about him?

Let's eat, drink and be merry for tomorrow we die!

Yes, tomorrow we do definitely die. (To quote Benjamin Franklin, "In this world, nothing can be said to be certain except death and taxes."). And this brings us back once again to the Ultimate Gamble.

We can be cowards and ostriches, or simply wait and see – or we can consider our choices with care and attention. It's up to us. But how do we go about considering our options?

CHAPTER TWENTY-SEVEN

If there's a Creator, how do we know he's good? And what does 'good' mean anyway?

Let's look at our 50/50 gamble again. If Mr A is right and there is a Creator/God, how can we know what he/she/it is like? Is he recognisable? Is he, in fact, the stern, finger-pointing father-figure we have learned to think of, the old man with a long white beard (a bit like a bad-tempered Santa) who sits up in the sky and watches us all "from a distance"?

But if Mr B is right, there is no Creator/Father-figure and we are free, aren't we? Free to kill, maim, abuse, steal from and have sex with, anyone we choose – with no come-back apart from failure of that eleventh commandment "Thou shalt not be found out."

But honestly, how do we know God is good? Really know, I mean. He/she/it might be anything at all – a disengaged spirit that creates things and then leaves them to fend for themselves, a game-playing spirit that sports with us like the gods in Greek mythology?

What do we know about him/her/it after all?

Not a lot, if we rely on scientific formulae – or guesswork, or wishful thinking, or by simply ignoring the whole thing - but a great deal if we look at the historical evidence. And there is plenty of that. There is also geological evidence, and - often discounted when it shouldn't be – personal testimony.

From a purely philosophical point of view, Keith Ward's recent book "Why there almost certainly *is* a God" puts it beautifully.

"God," he writes, "is not limited by time and necessity..." He] necessarily exists, knows all possibles and is a creative mind...is free to be creative in many different ways...to bring new sorts of good things or states into being."

I have to admit that I didn't like the word *'good'* at first, until I realised that in this context it doesn't mean *'virtuous'* in the way we humans usually think of it. That has too many unpleasant associations – being a "goody-goody," "a do-gooder" or "too good to be true" with a hands-together sort of piety. (My husband once referred to it as "Too much sweetness and light." I knew what he meant).

In this case, as Keith Ward points out, *'good'* means desirable for its own sake. A Good Thing! If you had the power to choose between happiness or pain for yourself (a good thing or a bad thing), which would you choose? Unless you are a masochist (in which case I suppose pain would *be* your happiness) or sunk in your own interminable gloom, I wager you would choose happiness, i.e. The Good Thing. So if God is capable of bringing about whatever he likes – beauty or ugliness, love or hate, harmony or discard and cruelty- why would he choose the darkness, the hate, the disharmony and the ugliness? All painful things that come back and hit us!

Any God who is any kind of god at all (certainly one worth worshipping) will choose all the good things - perfect love, perfect beauty and perfect happiness – perfectly desirable things. *'Good'* things.

And if God is the first cause of the universe (necessary and eternal because without him we wouldn't be here) – and if he weren't dependent on something else for his own existence – why would he keep something going if he stopped liking what he had made. As an irritant he could ignore? Hardly! All any God who was an Eternal Cause would need to do is stop causing it – think it out of existence. Then Pow! It would all be gone, which includes Planet Earth.

But suppose he more than liked what he had created? Suppose he loved it deeply because he had made it, and made it especially with love in mind? What then? Love is something impossible to enjoy on one's own - it has to be shared, there has to be a *loved object*. So it makes perfect sense to me that the extraordinarily intelligent and complex creation called Homo Sapiens was evolved and developed for that very purpose – to share the beauty, wonder and awesomeness of the universe, simply because it *is* beautiful, wonderful and awesome.

If this is true, the extraordinarily intelligent being, Mankind, must have been created by God *for* God – for the sharing of love. And love is the very pinnacle of human emotions - the highest, most sublime state of existence.

So we do know quite a lot about God, after all – including why he must be '*Good*' – (in other words, the ultimate in desirability).

There are other pointers, but these depend not on philosophy but on the world's best-seller of all time.

CHAPTER TWENTY-EIGHT

"It's in the Book"

No-one knows when the first book of the Bible, Genesis, was written because records don't go back far enough, but the stories in many of them have been supported by geologists and historians. They are, in fact, the oldest and most complete continuous written records in history.

The story of creation has amused me for years, not because I take it literally (not being a seven-day creationist) but because according to the very first book of the Bible, the order in which the earth was brought about (with just one or two blips in chronology) is the same as the order in which our scientists, naturalists and geologists have told us the earth was in fact created.

In other words, how did the authors of Genesis know what was only discovered by scientists centuries later?

Many of the earliest books sound very bloodthirsty, with plenty of massacres and beheadings, and even some ethnic cleansing here and there, but they were written for the people of their time. These were brilliant at mathematics and astronomy and engineering (think of the pyramids and central heating) but mostly were simpler beings than our 21st century, man. With no real medical knowledge to speak of, death was an everyday matter, and when death is taken for granted violence can be accepted as normal. In terms of our human life on the planet, beings so many thousands of years ago were children compared to our sophisticated digitally-minded selves – not that we have advanced very far in other directions. Man seems to be very much what Man always was, despite the Rule Book.

The idea of God, though, as Creator and Father who guides and looks after his children, is a steady, unwavering theme through the whole of the early part of the Bible known as the Old Testament.

This theme occurs time after time after time. In fact it is underwritten. The Creator God is the main character in all of them. Since those records began God (Allah, Jehovah) is their *raison d'etre*. And throughout history prophets have popped up – mostly being derided and/or executed for their pains – to tell about this Father figure, and people have written their stories.

Obviously, some of the earliest books being almost, if not actually, pre-history, are often in the form of allegories. They are what people would have understood at the time, and if they were often war-like and brutal that too would have been understood at the time.

All this abruptly changed 2,000-odd years ago, however, when a man named Jesus of Nazareth arrived on the scene, thereby ushering in what is known as the New Testament, or the New Covenant. The Old had been leading up to the New and Jesus completed it. To Christians, he is the fulfilment of the past and the hope of the future. (The Biblical references are referred to later in Chapter 34).

Because of this man, we come to see God in a new light. Suddenly everything falls into place in a totally unexpected and exhilarating way. An exciting way.

So who was he, this man? And why did he have such a profound and lasting effect on our beliefs, our lifestyles and our calendars?

CHAPTER TWENTY-NINE

Ants in the Cosmos

I was sitting in my garden one sunny summer afternoon, watching the ants rushing about under my feet looking indescribably busy, when I had what is now described as an epiphany.

I had stretched out my foot, thinking that I only had to stamp on one of the ants to put a summary end to its busyness. And I wondered what the ant made of my feet, which would seem incomprehensibly huge and dangerous (and unpredictable) in its own view of things. Did it, I wonder, consider me or us at all, or were its energies and attentions solely fixed on the purpose of rushing about, whatever that was? I decided that, to ants in general, my feet were about as far removed from their orbit as thunderstorms and earthquakes are from ours, and just as uncontrollable.

Thinking about thunderstorms made me look upwards to the scudding white baby clouds, which looked as unthreatening as cotton wool buds. And I thought how small I was in relation to the sky above me, and how insignificant in the scale of things. Yet we were all made (roughly speaking) of the same matter. Boiled down to our essentials, we would all find ourselves constructed more or less out of the very same materials as each other.

My ant, the clouds and me, we were all made of *matter*.

All this pricked another memory. In the same series of television documentaries presented by the same scientist/ presenter, he had asked a very significant question. He had asked, in relation to the immensity of space, "Where in all this is God?"

In my days of wandering around in an idly confused fashion through a maze of possibilities, I had asked myself the same question. If there really were a God, then I assumed he would be everywhere, but *how* everywhere, and *in what way* everywhere?

My television scientist had talked about the fourth dimension as a realistic proposition. He had talked about a land so completely flat that there was no conception of an Up or a Down. The very idea would be impossible for us to comprehend. The words would not be in our vocabulary. Then he asked us to Imagine that one day we'd be wafted upwards like paper in a sudden breeze, to come drifting slowly back down to earth. When we arrived, there would be no words to explain what had happened to us. No-one would believe us. They would think we were unhinged and recommend a good psychiatrist, whereas we would simply know we had been lifted up into a new dimension and had experienced marvels on the way.

At this point I had my epiphany, only in this case I jumped out of my deckchair (carefully avoiding any wandering ant) shouting "Bingo!"

Suddenly everything was clear as daylight.

God, I decided, is not made of matter, like us. How could he be? To create matter he had to be *outside* it, not *part* of it. God must be Pure Spirit – my presenter's personification of the fourth dimension. So it is not so much a question of "Where is God in all this?" as of "where *isn't* he?"

And the very fact of being wafted up into a region of Pure Spirit (which we all are from time to time, through beauty, awe and love) gives us experiences that are impossible to describe because there are no words for them. Poets, composers, and artists all have a crack at it, but no artists can ever convey exactly what they mean, nor are they ever truly satisfied with their work because it simply doesn't cover it.

So yes, those millions of us who have been wafted up from our own flat world and sailed slowly down again, seeing and hearing things indescribable in words, might well be considered unhinged.

There are plenty of people around (roughly two billion of them, according to Adherents.com. and more if we count

God believers of different faiths) who can testify to similar experiences. They have been there themselves and know what it's like. .

CHAPTER THIRTY

But where's the evidence?

Having decided that God was outside matter and therefore everywhere and anywhere, and that an all-powerful, all-intelligent Mind would only create desirable things for itself, I found myself wondering if there were any other evidence to say whether this Mind was really as loving and caring as he was said to be.

Sitting at my dressing table mirror deep in thought, I was preparing to plunge into a new day, and wondering how we could ever know for sure if he had our interests in mind. How could one ever know the real nature of God when he was so completely "other"?

The answer came to me, as usual, in one of those surprising shafts of light, rather like the sun coming suddenly through the clouds. The trouble, as I fully recognised, was that, although it was clear as crystal to me, the solution depended on my belief in the New Testament of the Bible – since the only truly personal knowledge of God open to us had to come through his humanity.

To a non-believer, my evidence was no evidence at all. Not scientific. Hardly worth quoting, in fact – except that it answered my own question in, to me, a perfectly logical way.

All I had, in fact, was the person God became – Jesus of Nazareth – and he was decidedly not the sort of man to create a bad joke and then leave it.

How did I know this? To describe this particular man properly would require the rest of this book – so I am merely going to suggest taking a dip or two into the records of four men called Matthew, Mark, Luke and John, who wrote about him personally and in detail. Only then are we in a position to make up our minds.

The dynamic man who strides through the pages turning traditional views on their heads, making friends with all the low life and upsetting the hierarchy rather rules out the "meek and mild" image we have been given for so long (and which has always infuriated me). Besides, he caused chaos in the temple by overturning all the commercial, 'animals-for-sacrifice' stalls because they were "turning God's house into a den of thieves" (Luke 19; 45-49). However right he was, I imagine running amok in your local meat market would need a fair amount of courage.

To accomplish all this, and to have thousands following him wherever he went, a man has to be irresistibly attractive, so since he was God's human face, God must be irresistibly attractive too!

So far so good! I was still staring blindly into the mirror when the further thought occurred, that since the Pure Spirit which occupies us and the space around us is timeless, ageless and not subject to the rules of matter, then the part of us which shares that spirit is also timeless, ageless and not subject to the rules of matter either.

Bingo again!.

I woke up and looked myself squarely in the face. Often in the past I have wondered why, no matter how many years we live and how old we grow, inside us we feel exactly the same as we've always felt. The sight of an ageing face with lines and sagging muscles comes as an endless and unpleasant surprise.

It was a surprise no longer. Because the spirit of Mary Frances is bound up with the Pure Spirit we call God, it exists in another dimension - out of reach of ageing skin and muscles. And if that dimension is God, then I have God within my own thinking, living, wondering self. What is more, so has everyone else who thinks and lives and wonders.

I laughed. "You may not believe in God," I said to the anonymous radio voice, "but according to my logic, you are walking around with him like the air in your lungs."

The idea was at once amusing and satisfying, for I

had only to look within me to find God – part of that ageless, timeless, essential *me* which would never grow old because it couldn't.

I would like to have been able to reply personally to the question "Where is God in all this?" put by our scientific presenter. I would have said: "Not Up There, or Out There, but *In Here!*"

So it's impossible for God to have left us. To someone who is beyond time and space and is everywhere, in everything, where else is there to go?

CHAPTER THIRTY-ONE

A Matter of Life and Death

Everything made of matter has to die. Even the stars implode or explode after their allotted spin in space. And even if things reform themselves eventually, they still have to die first.

Flowers struggle up through the earth from microdot seedlings to become astonishingly beautiful objects, all different from each other but all with a purpose of their own – even if most of us don't know what that is. Then, when their days of glory are done, they fall apart (literally – bits drop off) and wither into compost.

It shouldn't surprise us, then, that every human being must die at some point. Think of all the babies being born at any given moment. If nobody died, even with only the very minimum birth rates we would now be standing three deep on each other's heads. And how about the trillion upon trillion of animals, plants and humans that have ever inhabited Earth? Common sense alone tells us that the life/death cycle is not only understandable but unarguable. Where on earth would we be without it?

The question is: are all these plants, animals and humans the result of a quite extraordinary carbon-based accident, or did a Super-Mind create them all?

If life and death are accidental, the accident is astonishingly efficient. Think about it: Every plant, insect, bird and mammal has its own reproductive system. Each one has its own digestive system and food sources. And all are interdependent, so that taking one away is disaster for all the rest.

I believe in co-incidence, but to me 'accidental' is a step too far in the co-incidence stakes. And even now there are plenty of money-grabbing entrepreneurs happy to ignore the dependence we have on everything else. Too many trees cut down in a rainforest means flooding and soil erosion, the destruction of uncounted forms of wildlife and the livelihood of a whole native population – yet Big Business seems not to care. Do these tycoons really not care, or are they simply greedy and short-sighted?

Obviously they have never heard of Specsavers.

However, if we only have one chance of life, with nothing to look forward to afterwards, it would seem only fair to make the most of it. Enjoy it while we have it – even if it means killing off any other form of life that gets in our way.

If we are accidents, who cares what happens to all the other accidents?

On the other hand, if a Super-Mind caused all this amazingly effective and orderly cycle, then we have even more reason to enjoy our own span, pleasure, pain and all. And if all this beauty really were given to us to be enjoyed, we have a responsibility to nurture it. It's ours – so we'd better look after it.

If we truly believe that, we will not only be filled with awe for the wonder of Nature but we will be *grateful*.

And if after all there is 'something else' after death, then dying is just the door to this 'somewhere else.'

Remember the saying; "What goes around comes around?" It certainly works in life. Why not in the 'somewhere else' too?

Maybe it's a thought worth thinking.

Personal Note: Many years ago, when I was 18, I was torn between three possible careers. My father wished me to go to Art College, my Mother would have liked me to continue training as a possible concert pianist, but all I had ever really wanted to do, deep down, was write. My sister Paddy had just died at the age of 24. She and I had been very close, and I still felt I could talk to her. So one morning I asked her to tell me what to do, as decision time was approaching fast.

A few days later, my mother came into my bedroom early one morning, to say a Polish friend in London had rung with a strange

message. Our friend knew me as one of the Gorman girls, but knew nothing more – certainly nothing whatever to do with my personal life, present or future. She had phoned my mother because she had dreamed of Paddy the night before.

Paddy, she said, had stood at the end of her bed and smiled at her. "Tell Mary to practise her writing," she had said. My mother asked if that meant anything to me. "Yes," I said, "I asked her."

Whether my mother was surprised or not I never knew because we never spoke of it again, but this dream came as no surprise to me. I had asked my sister, my closest confidante, for help and she had provided it. What could be more natural?

It was only later that I fully realised the true significance of it all. If I, or a member of my family or close friend, had had that dream, it would have been natural and understandable - and open to the accusation of wishful thinking. A total stranger, on the other hand, would not have recognised my sister for who she was. It had to be someone who knew my identity but very little more – certainly not my dearest wishes (no-one knew those but myself at that particular moment). And it had to be transmitted via my mother, who saw my future in terms of music or art.

From that moment my life was re-designed. In those days there were no university courses for creative writing, and I knew I must always be within sight and reach of books. So I started work as a library assistant in Nottingham Public Libraries, where I met my future husband and became the proud mother of two talented and intelligent and most beloved sons.

So even when I had lost sight of God, believed "religion" to be a load of rubbish and dropped out of the church world altogether, even then I knew without doubt that death was not – could not be – the end. For otherwise how could Paddy have known of my dilemma, and how else could she deliver her message except through an intermediary who knew just enough but no more?

I took her advice, of course. I have been writing something-or-other ever since.

CHAPTER THIRTY-TWO

Slings and Arrows

One of the chief arguments *against* God, put forward by every atheist or agnostic I personally have ever met, is "If there is a good and loving God, why is there so much suffering in the world? Why does he allow all these wars and disasters?" Even more often, "Why has he done this to me?"

Good question, and one that Christians traditionally tended to slide out of by calling it a mystery. Well yes, no-one doubts it is a mystery. How can it be anything else, since God is not human (contrary to general belief - most people feel they would have made a much better job of it themselves if given the chance!)? But to a nonbeliever that answer is no answer at all. Rather like replying to a child's "why?" with "Because I say so."

If you are a non-believer the question is irrelevant anyway. There is no God so there can be no reasons for suffering except for the randomness of chance, or the weakness of our human bodies. Death, if scientists are clever enough in the future, can (some of us hope) be delayed or even outwitted - and wars and natural disasters are simply phenomena we have to endure until we have learned enough about nature (and of course politics and psychology) to stop them ourselves.

Really?

We don't seem to have progressed very far in the way of stopping either wars or disasters, despite many centuries of "learning about Nature." In fact, I am given to understand that the 20th century saw more wars than any other century in the past! Not a sparkling record, I'd have said.

If you are a God believer, however, the whole perspective changes. It is a mystery because God is 'other' – an infinite Mind totally unfathomable by our tiny, finite ones. As well may my ant try to work out my reasons by its own ant-ish rules. However intelligent and looked-up-to it may be in its own ant world, it will never even begin to understand mine because *it is an ant* and *I am a human being.*

As an argument that's fine, but only if you believe in a Creator God in the first place. Not enough, certainly, for our secular 21st century society.

The other aspect, which also presupposes a God, is the little matter of Free Will. If God created us because he wanted to, out of love, then he obviously wants *us* to choose *him* out of love. Who wants puppets? Love has to be a free choice. This means we are free to kill, maim, defraud and despoil as much as we like. The decision is entirely ours. God can't interfere unless we ask him – however much he wishes to - because he is bound by his own rules. Free Will is a gift he has given and can't take back.

According to those rules, then, if politicians invent weapons of mass destruction, or if suicide bombers blow themselves up on buses *don't blame God*. Blame the politicians and the suicide bombers.

As for tsunamis and earthquakes, they are part of the world we inhabit. They have always been there. They are, in fact, what caused our spectacularly beautiful landscapes, so maybe we should be more careful where and how we build our cities (e.g. not on the sides of volcanoes or on fault lines) or how we cut down swathes of irreplaceable forests for temporary gain – thereby not only eating our own seed corn but causing floods or drought.

Besides, we've already agreed we all have to die. Whether we go slowly and painfully of cancer or all together in an earthquake, the result is exactly the same. Someone goes – where? – and someone else is left behind to grieve.

That is going to happen eventually, whatever we may say or do about it

We might as well get used to the idea.

CHAPTER THIRTY-THREE

But how about pain?

Of course there's the hoary old question of pain.

What is so impossible about the idea that this earth is a training ground, a university? If our spirits really are part of the eternal Pure Spirit which is God - then our university (earth) may well be a place where we take on the struggles and hardships of life in this world in order to strengthen our spirits and help others to strengthen theirs.

Hard to understand?

Think of it as like soldiers being trained for battle, or a student studying for a Masters degree or a tennis player practising for a Grand Slam. All those demand hard work, struggle, sacrifice and usually a great deal of pain. But the soldiers/students/athletes are ready and happy to endure it. It's a means to an end, after all – to the medals, trophies, prize money and a wonderful sense of achievement.

There is absolutely no doubt that every single one of us suffers at some time or another. Even the tycoons, the highest of high achievers and the owners of mansions have their problems. Bereavement, ill health, disgrace, painful or accidental death, these are not restricted to the poor. The fact that the poor apparently have less material resources to cope with them (i.e. private medicine, private schools, expensive lawyers to keep the law at bay) strikes home to all of us, but to Faith followers this will all be balanced out at the end of life. ("Blessed are the poor, for theirs is the Kingdom of God" – the Beatitudes, Luke chap 6 v 20). There is also the lovely story of Lazarus at the rich man's gate, one of Jesus' own parables – told to the crowd as an illustration. (Luke 16: 19-31)

Lazarus, he said, was a beggar full of sores who spent his time sitting at a rich man's gate, hoping for scraps. Dogs came and licked Lazarus' sores, but the rich man ignored him and simply carried on enjoying the good things of life as if the beggar weren't there. When Lazarus died he was carried off by the angels to the comfort of Abraham's arms, but when the rich man died he found himself in Hades.

He called out to Abraham, asking if Lazarus could dip his finger in water to cool his tongue, but Abraham said he was afraid that wasn't possible. So instead, the rich man asked if Lazarus could be sent to warn his father and brothers of the fate that awaited them. At that, Abraham explained that Moses and the prophets had already done so but they hadn't been believed.

"No," said Lazarus, "but if someone came back from the dead to warn them they would definitely repent", to which Abraham replied that if his father and brothers hadn't believed what Moses and the prophets had told them, then they wouldn't believe even if someone did rise from the dead.

(How very true! Christians firmly maintain that Jesus did in fact rise from the dead, but, as he predicted in this story, not everybody believes them).

As for the pain and hardship we all suffer here and now, if we suffer them at our university, then, who is to blame? Certainly not God. Like any good parent, he simply wants to see us overcome them all and win our medals.

The "Why me?" question is soon answered. "Why not me? It happens to everyone else. What makes me so different?"

As for allowing wars and killings and the basic inhumanity-to-man we all despair of, the 'no puppets' rule comes into play here in a big way. Try forcing someone to love you and see how far it gets you! You will be shown the door.

Political democracy, after all, follows the same rule - that we should not have our individual freedoms taken away and abused by totalitarian dictatorship. It seems to me that the difference between slings and arrows as allowed by God, and the same slings and arrows caused by man or by accident, is that the one gives us a *reason* for them while the other one doesn't.

Put simply – Science tells us *how* things are.
God tells us *why*.

Personal Note: An intriguing thought - Could it also be possible that we have all volunteered to come? Signed up as students? That is certainly an interesting theory all by itself, because, if true, people who say: "I didn't ask to be born" may just possibly be wrong. Perhaps they did ask to be born. Can anyone prove otherwise?

CHAPTER THIRTY-FOUR

Is Jesus a Myth?

Was Jesus just a good man, or just another prophet?

Was "Christ" his surname?

Why should we believe he existed at all?

Why indeed? Except that he is in our history books. The 1st Century historian, Josephus, mentioned him in *Antiquities of the Jews*. His words have been dissected and argued over for centuries but, whatever the controversy, there is no doubt that five different historians, Josephus, Tacitus (*annals*), Suetonius (*lives of the Caesars*), Thallus and Pliny all tell us that Jesus lived, performed surprising works and was finally crucified. Christians are referred to by most of them as "a tribe which exists to this day".

Considering that "this day" was more or less 2,000 years ago and that the Christian tribe still continues to proliferate around the globe, is something academics can argue about to their hearts' content but cannot *argue away*.

They can also conduct their polite battles over whether or not the accounts are all authentic, but the fact that at least five historians mention either Jesus or the Christian tribe certainly suggests some authenticity to me. (But then, I am a simple soul, who likes her two plus two to equal four).

There are also four main records of his life and death in the second half of the Bible, i.e. the New Testament. Matthew, Mark, Luke and John may not have agreed on all details, but the main plank of the story is precisely the same in all of them.

The very fact that these occasional inconsistencies are often used as an argument against the writers has always amused me. My sister and I can witness the same incident or be at the same function, and our separate accounts will vary enormously.

We will register different details according to who we are, like looking at the same view from different windows. In fact, I believe the police are suspicious of completely identical stories from different witnesses. They suspect collusion. So why should poor Matthew and the others not be allowed to remember different things?   How unfair we are!

There are other records in documents like the Dead Sea Scrolls and the Coptic Gospels, but since I personally haven't read these I wouldn't dare to comment on them.

Geologists, digging for clues in Israel, Palestine and the surrounding area, have uncovered artefacts that confirm many of the records. And even the other main religions acknowledge the fact that Jesus really did live and die at that time.

Even the dating of our calendars, for the most part worldwide, starts from the supposed date of Jesus' birth, A.D. (*Anno Domini - After Christ*).

What's more, 2,000 years later people are still prepared to die for him, only preferably not by killing other people first. Any so-called Christians who do kill are most definitely not following their leader, who in fact advocated turning the other cheek – not to mention the 5th D I Y Rule, "No killing."

There is, in fact, more documentation about Jesus than there is of King Alfred, let alone his cakes! The Dark Ages are called that because we know so little about them. Yet we are taught to believe all those. I certainly was, anyway, when I was at school.

We are certainly not taught to write them off as myths.

So why do we fight what seems to be an unarguable fact?

A man called Jesus lived and died. He is quite evidently not a myth.

As for being just a good man or just another prophet, in saying the things he did he must have been either insane (which he clearly wasn't), a liar prepared to die an excruciating death for his lies, or he was genuine. In other words, he had to be either mad, bad or telling the truth.

No-one so far has ever suggested he was bad. Even non-believers say he was a "good man," whose wisdom has survived until now.

There are even indications in the Old Testament that the Jews' long-awaited Messiah would, in fact, be Jesus himself, (Psalms 2 v 1-12; 16 v 9-11; 22 v 16-18; 118 v 22-29. Genesis 49 v 10; Zechariah 12 v 10).

The trouble was that although the Jews were expecting a Saviour, they were looking for a rather different *kind* of Saviour. They were expecting someone to come *in glory* to defeat their foes and save them from domination by Rome. He was to be a proper, regular sort of *king,* not a carpenter, a nobody, from a village called Nazareth. To add to their difficulties, this man's attitude was shockingly different from their own. He ignored petty rules and healed people on the Sabbath (shock, horror!), and scandalized them by partying with the lowest of the low (you couldn't get much lower than prostitutes and tax collectors at the time).

It was all very hard to handle, so in the end they killed him off. He was a heretic, a blasphemer and, worst of all, a *troublemaker* who could cause them grief with their Roman masters. Unfortunately for them, although they had obviously killed him, he didn't behave properly even then. He should by rights have stayed dead. But according to the many witnesses who met and talked to him afterwards, he came back to life again.

On that fact lies 2,000 years of the faith known as Christianity.

Not only his words and actions through his life, but his words and actions after he had died – all these together make up what we know about Jesus the Man – and, even more importantly – what we know about his father, God the Creator.

"I am in the Father and the Father is in me," he declared: "He who has seen me has seen the Father." (John chap. 14 v 7-11). Therefore looking at Jesus tells us all about God.

Unfortunately this only works if you come down on the side of a Creator rather than that of Chemical Accident. What's more, it all requires more than just written evidence, or even the witness of many millions of people.

It requires something that many modern scientists dismiss as an aberration, a regrettable delusion. It requires *personal experience.*

Personal Note: If you would like to know what Jesus was really like, and before dismissing him as "just a good man" or a fraudulent shyster, I recommend the four gospel stories of Matthew, Mark, Luke and John, as well as the account called the Acts of the Apostles which follows them. As adventures go, these five action-packed stories beat anything our modern culture can offer.

Christ was not his surname. The word means "Messiah", so really he is Jesus the Messiah, or Jesus the Christ. He real name would have been Jesus bar Joseph (of Nazareth)

Incidentally, the word "gospel" means "Good News." Worth a try?

CHAPTER THIRTY-FIVE

The Relationship

For the true Christian – of whichever denomination – the Church is not a building or a creed to be followed. It isn't laws to be obeyed or even a carrot-and-stick set of superstitions.

It is a *relationship*.

It is unconditional love from a Creator God who loves us *no matter what*. Because he loves us enough to take on human form and die for us, then all we can do is love him back.

Christians believe (know!) that this man Jesus died in excruciating agony and in the most humiliating circumstances, to be the ultimate sacrifice. Instead of killing lambs or doves he allowed himself to be killed in their place, and by doing so he restored our own relationship with his father – the Creator God. *"He became what we are so that we may become what he is."* (St Athanasius)

This belief (knowledge) is as real to the true Christian as knowledge that our sons and daughters are our in fact our sons and daughters – that the television screen in the corner of the living room is capable of giving us the news, the cup final and Strictly Come Dancing.

The question is, how do we arrive at this relationship? Is it a privilege enjoyed by the few? Is it a mental aberration, a fault in one of our brain cells? Or is it the particular rite of an ancient society which simply has to worship something?

The true answer is astonishingly simple. *We ask for it.*

Personal Note: I was once at a dinner party, sitting next to a well-dressed, prosperous-looking young man. He noticed the cross I wore (still wear) and asked if it were simply decoration or whether it had any meaning for me. I told him yes, it had very definite meaning.

He leaned back in his chair to regard me with the kind of interest one might show a new species of buttercup.

"Would you like to know why you believe and I don't?" he asked.

I said yes, I would, very much.

"You believe and I don't because just here (and he tapped my head) you've got a part of your brain that believes in God and I haven't."

I smiled but didn't reply. A dinner party in a friend's house is not the best place to indulge in religious arguments. Besides, in those early days I hadn't the right words or sufficient confidence to explain what I meant. But if it happened now I would just love to point out that not having a faculty is usually regarded as a handicap. Having no kidney, or being blind or deaf is a subject for sympathy, not for boasting.

Amazingly, he showed no signs of envying me. In fact, he was obviously proud of his defect. I was the mutant, not he!

I would also ask him why any faculty is given at all if it has no purpose. Presumably this man had the ability to feel awe and wonder. If eyes are to see with and ears are to hear with, fingers to use as tools and nerve endings for pleasure or warning – and if kidneys, liver and intestines have their specific uses, why have we been given an entirely useless function? I would imagine that an organ designed specifically for worshipping would have a very specific purpose – to enable us to do just that – worship.

A pretty poor design it would be if there were nothing worth worshipping at the end of it!

Q.E.D?

I am, of course, biased. Having had a personal encounter with this worship-worthy someone I personally have no doubts.

CHAPTER THIRTY-SIX

Up close and personal

Have you ever been in love? I mean *in love,* not *in lust* – ready to die for the adored person, to give him/her the moon and stars and want nothing more than to talk about the beloved forever and ever to whoever is prepared listen? If so, you will know that the experience is totally, entirely, wholly, indescribable – and probably inexplicable to people who haven't been there. ("Can't think what all the fuss is about – it's only a man/woman/hormones after all!")

Can anyone really and honestly explain the phenomenon? The fact of 'falling in love' does have a scientifically explained, hormonal and practical aim – without it we would all die out. But Love itself? Not just the sexy one but the love of parent for child, for friend for friend, for husband and wife after the hormones have calmed down a bit? Even love for one's country, or for a pet dog or cat (or rabbit or horse, one can go on and on)? This has proved impossible to explain scientifically because no matter how clever we are we can't cut it out and slice it up and put it under a microscope.

How about Beauty? The ravishing sight of Autumn trees, of the sun slipping gloriously behind a seascape. How about the enchantment of music, the wonder of inspired paintings, or simply the boneless grace of kitten-and-puppyhood?

My dinner party neighbour was right in that we can know which part of the brain is active at any one time. We can even can say it's responsible for our thoughts and actions. But if we took it out we would be none the wiser. We still wouldn't be able to *see* it working.

Abstract knowledge is cold. Relationships are warm, living things. So excluding explanations other than purely scientific ones seems, to my inescapably 'sensible' brain, to be totally missing the point.

At least half, if not a great deal more, of our responses are inspired by emotions – not thoughts at all. By feelings of hope, resentment, hatred, envy, joy or fear.

Of course, not being medically or scientifically trained, I am ready to be told that taking away part of our brain would leave us incapable of certain thought processes, but so far as I can see, it wouldn't take away our capacity to feel emotion. We are not robots. And ignoring the existence of rage and hate could lead us into severe trouble.

So where do those responses come from?

To appreciate nature, beauty and music, even scientists agree that we need something extra.

Personal experience.

That is where our Pure Spirit comes in again. A spirit cannot be weighed or numbered, finger-printed or have its DNA recognised. It simply has to be experienced.

What the combined Spirit of Jesus and his Creator Father offers to everyone (not just the 'good' ones) is the *something extra*. Because Jesus is the accessible, human face of God, all we have to do is ask him to come in. (*"Here I am. I stand at the door and knock; if anyone hears my voice and opens the door I will come in and will dine with him, and he with me." – Revelation 3:20*)

That's all very well, but what happens then?

If you dare to take the chance, the result will change your life. You will be empowered, inspired, motivated and given what nothing else in the world can offer you.

Joy!

Real joy that has nothing to do with winning the Lottery but everything to do with sheer, unmitigated delight. And peace, the internal sort that carries on being there even in the darkest places.

It will also present you with a challenge! Being a Christian will never prevent bad things happening to you. On the contrary you will need support, mostly because it takes courage to stand up for your beliefs in a secular world. Having other Christians on hand, though, plus the peace and joy, courage and compassion that only God can give you, sees you through.

Besides, you will be so 'in love' with this relationship that you may even be accused of being inebriated. (You wouldn't be the first. On the Day of Pentecost when all the terrified disciples were suddenly intoxicated with courage, everyone thought they *were* drunk). Of course you may also become a bore to the unlucky ones who haven't had the Spirit of God hit them on the head, but that is the risk you and they will have to run!

I know all this because this Spirit of God undoubtedly hit me on my head in 1978 and my life was changed forthwith. It gave me a joy I had never experienced – and not just for a while either. It lasts to this day, even when I may be feeling miserable about something else.

Don't just take my word for it (as if you would!). Take a good look at the evidence and decide for yourselves.

Personal Note: According to some scientists, people who say they have 'experienced' God are victims. Such experiences are, to them, the result of a malfunction somewhere - ideas picked up from other people, maybe, in a sort of mob hysteria. Or of impressionable minds reading or seeing the wrong things at the right moments.

But does this explain the billion or so Christians (I don't know the precise number of Muslims, Sikhs, Hindus and Buddhists around the globe) who not only believe in their God but declare they know Him and have a relationship with Him?

Asking for a personal conviction, however, is a bit like leaping into space, we can't be sure someone is going to catch us until we've done it.

CHAPTER THIRTY-SEVEN

Magic wands?

One thing I can definitely vouch for is that God answers our requests, even if we don't recognise the answers straight away.

We can call miracles by plenty of other names – magic, coincidences, synchronicity or "things that would have happened anyway". We can even follow instructions in our book of spells, and gather eyes of newt and legs of frogs, turn round three times under a full moon, or stick pins in little wax figures. (I personally haven't tried that, but it seems to require a great deal of trouble and effort for debatable results).

But when we get a thousand coincidences following a thousand requests for them (to the Supermind we call God) which stop when the requests stop, then for me that becomes too much of a coincidence!

I can quote from personal experience (and am always happy to do so), and could continue to quote more and more as time goes by, but lists are boring and there are plenty of people who can testify to the truth that *"Ask and you shall receive"* is not merely an empty promise.

But what of prayers that don't seem to get answered? What of the mothers who pray for their soldier son's safety and are then told of his death? Or the innocent victims of war and famine, praying for rescue? Or even the prayers for specific jobs that are then given to other people.

All those things happen. The question is why?

One answer is "trust," which sounds all too easy and might well be termed a 'cop-out.' Just another mystery quoted by Christians who have no other answers. However, in my experience, trust *works*. If one believes in a loving Father God who has everyone's best interests at heart, it becomes quite possible to see the end (what happens after death) as addressing every problem we might have had when we were alive. Sometimes – quite often, in fact – the problems we see now as disasters resolve themselves into unexpected benefits. We might have ended up hating the job we applied for with such hope. Maybe the man or woman who let us down would have made the worst possible partner for us. And if our sons or daughters hadn't died when they did, they might have suffered the deepest unhappiness through all their lives.

When I look back to what I thought at the time were disasters, I can see that they eventually brought me to a better position than I was in before. If I hadn't lost all my money, I would not be where I am now – in the perfect situation to write books. If I hadn't suffered the trauma of divorce I would not have found independence or discovered true friendship in other ways. And if I hadn't been through disbelief and enough sins to fill ten books, I would not be capable of writing this particular book now.

I have named only three "ifs" but there are vastly more, I promise you.

To form any kind of relationship with God leads inexorably to trusting – that God will answer our requests in the best possible way for us in the end.

After all, he created us for love, and love delights in giving things.

As for the magic wand aspect, Hogworts has nothing on God for producing extraordinary results. My own story, *The Song of the Spinning Sun* describes a few of them.

Personal Note: A story - A man once died and was taken first to hell, where there were long tables full of people trying to eat a sumptuous meal with spoons that were so long they couldn't bring them near enough to their mouths. Everyone was frustrated and starving. The man was taken next to heaven, where he saw exactly the same tables full of people with the same food and the same long spoons, but in this case no-one was hungry because they were all feeding each other!)

Another story: Have you heard about the climber hanging on desperately to the side of a cliff who calls out "Is there anybody there?"

A voice replies "Yes, let go and you will be safe."

After a short silence, the climber calls again "Is there anybody else there?"

And another: Then there's the story of the man caught in a flood who takes refuge on his rooftop and calls out to God to rescue him. A canoe comes past but he refuses help because, he says, "God is going to rescue me".

Shortly afterwards a large motorboat passes below and offers him a lift, but again he refuses because God is going to rescue him. Last of all, a helicopter hovers overhead, but the man is still convinced that God will do the trick.

When he's finally left alone he cries out to God: "Why haven't you rescued me?" and the Lord replies: "Well, I've sent you a canoe, a motorboat and a helicopter, what more do you want?"

What more do we want? What will really convince us that matter is not everything there is?

CHAPTER THIRTY-EIGHT

The Ultimate Scandal -
Divide and Rule

One of the reasons why Christianity isn't taken seriously in the UK is the hoary old truth "Divide and Rule," which gets more and more true as time goes on.

Because Christians, all over the world but mostly in the UK, have divided themselves up into denominations, all thinking they alone know the door to God and Jesus and Heaven, we spend too much time defending *our own particular door*, instead of the God and his Son we all profess to believe in.

Why?

To true Christians there can be no 'door' to God, except the one where he stands knocking, hoping we will open it. God came to us instead. He turned himself into a human being for 30 or so years, and made himself available to us *at all times*. It was a case of his life for ours!

He is the great forgiver of the past, hope for the future and help in the present. He is the same for all of us, whichever church we happen to attend. So why not say so?

Are we such cowards that we cannot get together in one united front to proclaim our faith to a secular world, as the Muslims do? Are we so closed-minded that we cannot see that the bottom line of our faith is exactly the same whichever denomination we adhere to? Or that our divisions, bigotry and misunderstandings are a scandal to the rest of society?

We don't have to be all the same. We can all go to the communities that suit us best – noisy, reflective, simple or full of ritual and ceremony. Why shouldn't some people enjoy their 'smells and bells' when others are enjoying their quiet simplicity? What harm do we do to each other?

Let's pool our resources instead, forget and forgive past

animosities, celebrate where we agree, and stand up for our communal faith.

Personal Note: As a perfect illustration of how togetherness works, I was one of the few Roman Catholics encouraged to attend "Mission England", Billy Graham's visit to the UK in 1984. We volunteer counsellors, from all the denominations, went through training sessions first, then interviewed to make sure we were all singing from the same hymn sheet. What astonished and impressed me was that the training given was the bottom line Christianity in which we all believed, and to which we all agreed. We were told that each new person going forward at Billy Graham's invitation was to be asked which church they came from, if any, and which they would prefer to attend. They were all sent to the churches of their choice.

To me this was a revelation. In 1984, nicely counteracting George Orwell's best-selling and extraordinarily depressing book, the Church had got it right.

Can we not take heart and inspiration from Mission England?

CHAPTER THIRTY-NINE

Rogues, Mavericks and Whacky Fanatics

It's fairly obvious that murdering whole populations just isn't right or even sensible, whatever the reason. And when the reason given is that their faith isn't the same as ours, it becomes less so than ever – downright stupid in fact. Yet there are, and have always been, enough fanatics to do it, and with our wonderful electronic gadgets there are now even more ways of carrying it out.

Unfortunately, fanatics don't have to resort to mass murder to do their damage. Take the rather embarrassing question of the whackier evangelists who pin us in corners and wave highly coloured literature under our noses – especially if they are bigoted and misinformed.

Happily, there are countries in the world (notably the USA, Brazil and Mexico, which have the highest percentage of Christians to population – see page 39) where talking about the historical figure of Jesus bar Joseph, carpenter of Nazareth, is not only *not* embarrassing but comfortably normal and everyday.

Not so in the UK. Unfortunately, the British temperament being what it is, anything that smacks of emotionalism is avoided like Swine flue. Except when it comes to Football matches, of course, or The X Factor, or gigs by Status Quo, jumping up and down and screaming one's adoration is (shudder!) something a good English person *does not do*. And anyone who forces us to do so will get the good old English cold shoulder, with their victims staring into unlikely shop windows or slipping quietly down side streets to avoid contamination.

Why is that?

Why is it that Muslims can walk proudly in their enveloping robes and pray openly three, four or five times a day, proclaiming their beliefs clearly to our interested (and often deeply impressed) eyes, without censure, while one or two brave Christians can stand alone and avoided on street corners, handing out literature which no-one wants to accept in case someone sees them and – horror of horrors – laughs!

There are football addicts who travel across country, and often across continents, in order to scream at matches where eleven men are kicking a football from one end of a field to the other with varying degrees of skill. And programmes where people who win fortunes are greeted with screams of delight while the winners sob and hug everyone within arms reach.

Yet church services where believers sing tuneful, singable songs and even (gasp!) raise their hands in the air, are dismissed by traditional worshippers as 'happy clappy.' Beneath consideration of 'normal', respectable English churchgoers.

It doesn't make sense, does it?

Everyone believes in something. Whether we are Christians (of any denomination), Jews, Muslims, Sikhs or Buddhists, humanists or atheists, we all have a faith of some kind. The trouble only comes when believers in one faith insist that theirs is the only faith possible, which is where the mavericks and whacky fanatics come in.

We can become out-and-out zealots and fundamentalists, happily killing off the odd hundred people here and there to prove a point – their particular point, of course. In these cases the rogues, mavericks and fanatics have obviously lost track of the original cause they were fighting for. They have, in fact, simply missed the point and lost the plot.

I am of course speaking about *irrational* enthusiasts. Enthusiasm for *rational* (good) causes is something else again, and to be applauded. There are, however, plenty of the other kind, past and present. Remember the Holocaust and the Crusades? But in all these cases they were and still are obeying their own laws, following causes that seem only too rational to them at the time.

Their own laws, that is, not God's.

Unfortunately, they can do horrifying damage that may take centuries to repair.   They are often acting on a twisted version of genuine beliefs handed down to them by others. But I strongly suspect that they are mainly motivated by politics whether they realise it or not - and mostly they don't.

When all's said and done, the political motive applies to 'religious' wars all over the globe. In order for power politics to flourish (which of course it does, wherever human beings find themselves – from mud hut to penthouse) the inhabitants are encouraged to pin the whole thing on their god(s) and to fight to the death in what is often a never-ending cause. And, as we've already seen, there are more than enough gods to go round for that purpose (the Science God being the newest kid on this block).

Most rogues and mavericks, however, do other things besides try to kill off the opposition. They do their damage more subtly – mostly, I fear, to their own causes.

Fundamentalist Christians, fundamentalist Muslims, fundamentalist anything at all – can wield the big "DO NOT" sticks, the sticks of bigotry, rigid non-forgiveness and lack of love. From the truncheons of despotism, expulsion and martyrdom down to the twigs of contempt and harassment.

To Christians, God is Love.

Whatever is not done in love is incompatible with the God of love himself.

CHAPTER FORTY

The only two D I Y Rules that matter

According to Jesus of Nazareth, who always spoke according to God (who happened to be his father, so he should know) all the Ten Commandments (D I Y Rules) can be reduced to two:

Love God, and love your neighbour as yourself. The Golden Rule, in fact.

When you think about the ten, this makes perfect sense. The first are all about loving God and not using his name profanely. But all the rest are to do with treating other people with respect, from our parents down to our next door neighbours – even, I'm sorry to say, to the guy down the street who lets his dog foul our front gardens, or the woman in the office who tells tales about us when we're out of the room.

These people may give us ulcers or have us dreaming sweet thoughts of revenge, but we still have to treat them with respect because to do anything else will in the end lead to even more trouble - and yet more ulcers.

As we have already seen, 'Own back, own back' *doesn't work.*

Even more importantly, if we believe that God loves them *as well as* us, how can we not do the same?

Easier said than done? Yes of course. But have you noticed that nothing really worthwhile is ever easy? Wallpaper put straight onto walls not properly primed and prepared doesn't stick. Paint over layers of old paint never looks smooth and has to be redone. Students who never do their homework fail their exams. And athletes who spend more time in the pub than in training never win races.

Loving one's neighbour takes practice and is just about impossible without help. But there is a wise adage that says:

"Make a friend out of your enemy and you have lost your enemy."

If we all did that, there would be no need for the last six or seven commandments. They are written into the script!

Personal Note: Please note that the commandment is to love our neighbour as ourselves, not more, not less, but equally. But that means loving ourselves in the first place.

How do we do it? How about "If God loves us, who are we to argue?"

The Golden Rule is acknowledged by all major religions. In Buddhism: "Hurt not others in ways that you yourself would find hurtful."(Udana-Varga 5,1). Hinduism (Mahabharat 5,1517). Islam: "None of you is a believer until he desires for his brother that which he desires for himself"(Sunnah). It is also written in the Mosaic Law, so there is nothing new in this commandment.

CHAPTER FORTY-ONE

Why me?

How can God love me when there are so many other people in the world who need his love more than I do? Why should he focus on me – or you – or anyone in the West who has enough to eat?

The idea came to me one day while I was sitting up in bed drinking my morning cuppa, and I couldn't wait to write it down.

Take a grain of sand. One tiny grain doesn't have to be joined to another grain to become sand. It already *is* sand. A massive stretch of it doesn't make it any more sand than it was before. One grain is complete in itself and the stretch is simply called 'a beach'.

The tiniest droplet of water doesn't need any help from other drops in order to become water. It already *is* water. And a vast stretch of it isn't any more water than it was already – it is complete in itself, and the mass is simply called 'the sea'.

So God's love isn't one entity to be shared among trillions of needy people. Being entirely spirit, Love isn't made of matter - yet the principle is the same. Unfortunately we don't have a word that covers it (for the sake of argument, call it 'drop') but one drop of love doesn't make it any less 'love' than an oceanful. It is complete in itself. So one drop of God's love is as enveloping and totally focussed as the oceanful of it that we call God.

If this is true, then you and I are as much loved as the elderly woman in Zimbabwe trying to bring up her three orphaned grand-children. Or the prisoner of conscience held and tortured in a secret place.

God loves them, but he also loves you and me.

What an amazing thought!

Personal Note: An even more amazing thought: God even loves the worst of the worst. A last-minute recognition of who God is enough to give us a fresh start. There's the parable of the workers in the vineyard (Matthew 20: v 1-16) where men who were given jobs at the very last minute were given the same wages as those who had been working hard all day. When these complained, his reply to one of them was "Friend, I am doing you no wrong. Did you not agree with me for one denarius? Take what is yours and go your way. I wish to give this last man the same as to you. Is it not lawful for me to what I wish with my own things? Is your eye evil because mine is good?" So we all have an equal chance in the end. My own opinion is that the more we give love in this life the more we will appreciate it when we meet it face to face.

Limitless Mind, Limitless heart

CHAPTER FORTY-TWO

The Mysterious Three

Everyone has trouble with the idea of the Holy Trinity – the concept of one God in three persons. The description of it as yet another Mystery seems to the non-believer to be yet another cop-out. One more "It's true because I said so" device to stem arguments from the Faithful.

The problem there is that so much of life really is a mystery that this one simply joins the ranks of all the scientific ones as well as the faith ones. Why should Science be allowed its unsolved questions while God is not allowed any at all?

I have personally wrestled with this one, but being mortal with my little finite, mortal brain, have never quite come up with the perfect solution. Probably because there isn't one. God is, after all, 'other.' *"For my thoughts are not your thoughts,, My ways are not your ways – it is the Lord who speaks." Yes, the heavens are as high above earth as my ways are above your ways, My thoughts above your thoughts." (Isaiah 55.6-9)*

I've thought of various ways to describe the phenomenon. There's the Doctor Joseph Smith, who is also my next-door-neighbour Joe, who at the same time is "Dad" Joe to his family. Three aspects of the same person.

There is also the Pure Spirit (God the Creator) with his human persona (Jesus of Nazareth, his son) and the force of love and power emanating from both (The Holy Spirit).

My favourite, though, is the illustration of a heart enclosing a three-leafed clover. God the Father Creator in one leaf, his son Jesus in another and the counsellor, their empowering Spirit, in the third - the whole joined together on one stem and wrapped securely and forever in Love.

The Creator is 'other' and needs an identifiable face. The

son can't be everywhere at the same time in human form without causing a sensation in the press (!), so the Counsellor has been given to us instead. The distillation of all wisdom, all power and all love, to empower us, to comfort and protect and guide and give us indescribable joy and peace.

A staggering thought! And all we have to do is accept it. If true, who in their right minds would turn down such an offer?

CHAPTER FORTY-THREE

In a nutshell

So where does all that leave us?

It depends, of course, on who we are and where we are standing. The only way to answer the question is to run through the points to see if they make sense.

Is there a Creator or are we accidents? Is it really a 50/50 matter?

Following my own brand of reasoning that two and two make four, it seems to me that there is no case to answer. If the earth and its contents (including our highly intelligent but often idiotic selves) have evolved from a combination of basic particles, there is still the unanswerable problem of *what started it all off?* In short, who or what caused the basic particles and the Big Bang?

If there is a Creator how do we know he's good?

There may be as many possible creators as there are human brains to imagine them, but there is only one for whom there are many thousands of years' worth of evidence – documentary, geological and spiritual. And this Creator could be described as a Super-mind capable of creating the very best out of an infinite number of possibilities. Not only the very best for himself but the best for the astonishingly intelligent beings he has evolved who are capable of appreciating the beauty and love he has created.

Are there rules for survival? Apart from sheer self interest?

Yes, ten – but only two that really matter - Love God and love each other as much as we love ourselves. To break these rules leads to pain, ultimately to destruction. Put your hands on a hotplate and you will suffer first-degree burns. Cross the road without looking and you will finish up in hospital – if not in the morgue. And running off with someone else's partner leads to hurt, bitterness and broken heads as well as hearts – not to mention bewildered and insecure children who secretly think it is all their fault.

Steal from other people and you will land yourself in gaol. Kill them and you face life sentences. And indiscriminate sex leads to hardening of the hearteries.

Who and why Jesus Christ?

If we believe in this good Creator, we will believe the documentary evidence - that he loves his creation (us) so much that he actually got himself born in order to save it/us from self-destruction. What's more, he died a hideous death under torture to bring this about – then came back to life again to show us that there really *is* life after death.

Plenty of witnesses wrote about seeing him alive and well when he was supposed to be dead and buried. He cooked a fish supper for them on the beach, and showed them the scars in his hands and feet and side from the torture.

If we believe these written reports, we will know that Jesus Christ is *still* alive and well – and with us forever. To die for someone has to be the ultimate expression of love. How do we repay the debt?

The answer to that is the same as ever – we repay in the only way we can. We accept it with love and gratitude. This is Super-love we are being offered and it's completely unconditional. It cannot be earned, only received.

How do we know he died to save us from condemnation and death?

Because he told us so. He came, he said, to give his life as a ransom for many by offering himself as a once-and-for-all sacrifice, in payment for all the things the human race has done wrong in the past (and continues to do in the present). Without his help, we are incapable of being the perfect human beings we would all like to be. But he knows this, and loves us anyway!

This is the good news (the gospel). By allowing himself to be tortured and atrociously killed, he has wiped the slate clean for the rest of us.

What news could possibly be better?

How do we get to know this 'alive and well' person who is also God? And what can he do for us?

There is only one answer I need to give. Open the door and invite him in. Everything else will follow.

Personal Note: Reading the New Testament is an experience in itself. The four stories of Jesus' life are mind-blowing, intensely moving and very exciting, while the Acts of the Apostles is the most exciting adventure story ever. All these open our minds to new possibilities – of deep, lasting happiness, a totally indescribable sense of peace and – best of all – HOPE!

Wow!

Personal Note: If the chances for God are 50/50, there is nothing to lose if we're wrong, but everything to gain if we're right.

A win/win situation in fact.

CHAPTER FORTY-FOUR

Our Future Leaders

It sounds trite to say that today's school children are tomorrow's prime ministers, chancellors of the exchequer, policemen and teachers – not to mention the most important influence of all, *parents* – but it happens to be true and should be considered.

What kind of world are we building for them and for ourselves? If we survive the environmental crisis, we will be left with others – one of which is the so far neglected question of what we're going to put into the bathwater now that the Faith baby is being thrown out.

Because it is such an important question, I felt it would be interesting to see what today's school children really thought about life. So I sent out 75 questionnaires to different schools, ages varying from 14 to 18. I received 50 replies back. Five of them were not completely filled in, but the rest were illuminating.

20 did not believe in a creator, 14 did, and the rest didn't know. Only seven went to church. Only four believed in a life after death. 25 thought there was a purpose in life, although mostly it was a material one. And all but two agreed there is widespread teenage depression – the causes of which varied wildly from the weather to exams, from adults not listening, to terrorism and global warning, and from drugs to racism and bullying. Three believed that teenagers in particular were depressed because they had no purpose, having left God out of the equation altogether (their words not mine).

The solutions to this depression varied, too. These went from the sublime to the bizarre (my favourites – "print more money" and "move to a warmer country". Delicious!) But all except one agreed we should respect each other regardless of individual circumstances.

Finally, 15 of my school children admitted to being influenced by their parents, seven by their peers and seven by both equally. Three said they were not influenced at all.

So if our parents form our first opinions, and if they are passing on a feeling of purposelessness, what kind of parents will these future politicians, civil servants, secretaries and engineers make?

Have we lost the plot again? An aimless society (apart from that of making as much money as possible in order to buy as many things as possible) will drift into confusion, and lose strength, power and motivation – and will ultimately collapse (think of the Roman Empire, the Aztec Empire, Stalin's communism, to name only three).

We are facing a global crisis in our climate. There are things we could and should be doing, but many of our leaders are choosing to play down the danger because they would lose money or power (those gods truly in action here). They remind me of a poker player on the supposedly unsinkable Titanic refusing to believe the ship is actually going down because he has a winning hand.

In exactly the same way, we are facing a spiritual crisis. To ignore the spirit which makes us all what we are is to ignore the greater part of ourselves – the part that *is!*

The great god Science is "non-proven" too. And to live without purpose is not Life but Existence!

A society without hope will grow sick and die.

Is this our wake-up call? I think so.

ROUND-UP

Since I shall undoubtedly be accused of bias, weighting the evidence in favour of a Creator God, I think I'd better finish with my own logical reasoning for doing so.

Is it truly a 50/50 gamble? Yes, it has to be since neither the Creator side nor the Faith side can ultimately prove their own arguments - for the simple reason that without actually dying and coming back to tell us, proving it is impossible. And even if we did, we wouldn't be believed.

Why have I chosen to bet on the Faith side? Because if the universe was formed with a big bang, we have to ask ourselves what caused the bang. And whatever caused it must be someone or something 'outside' the universe. Alien. Non-matter. Spirit. Had it been 'inside' it, something or someone would have had to cause it.

How do we know the First Cause is a 'good' something or someone – i.e., desirable? If an outside and limitless Mind can create anything it wants, it would presumably create something desirable in itself. Otherwise why bother?

Why Jesus? If our First Cause is desirable, creating desirable things, he/she/it must have created Mankind to be desired and desiring – and the only way to love and be loved is *freely*, otherwise it is mere puppetry. If Mankind chooses to abuse its free will and work against its creator, it will land itself in a mess. And the only way to point Mankind in the right direction again is to become human. Jesus is the human face of the Creator God.

Why did he have to die to save us? All gods, all religions, pagan or otherwise have demanded sacrifice. In some pagan religions the sacrifice was virgins or children. In the days of Jesus the Jews sacrificed birds or animals. At all times, the sacrifices had to be pure and spotless (hence the pagan virgins). Jesus, who was God and couldn't disobey his own instructions, allowed himself to be killed instead of the lambs and doves as a once-for-all sacrifice. Job done! Then he came back to life again, to be seen by many, many people.

How do I know it's all true and not a fable? Jesus bar Joseph, a carpenter from Nazareth, is well documented as having lived when he was suppose to live, and subsequently been crucified. As for the rest, there is too much documentation to be argued away. The four testimonies of his friends and disciples, plus the stories and letters that follow them, plus again the old scrolls found in caves, cannot be overlooked or denied.

So why do I believe in a limitless, all powerful, omnipresent God who loves us because we are his creation, made for loving? Because Jesus said so and if I believe in Jesus of Nazareth I therefore believe what he told me.

Is there another element to this belief? Yes, definitely. It's called Personal Experience and cannot be ignored or laughed out of existence any more than being in love can be ignored. If one falls in love with God, there is no way one can deny it.

Have I fallen in love with God? Yes, in 1978. Since then nothing has ever been the same. What's more, I have never been the same.

This logic is my own. I offer it merely as that, asking no-one to join me or even to agree with me. And if professional academics, or convinced atheists choose to laugh at my logic, well so be it. I have placed my bet and made my choice. You are all free to make your own.

All I ask is that you keep an open mind to the possibility that one of us maybe wrong.

Mary Frances

Thank you for listening.

Final Note

It is worth pointing out that choosing the God option doesn't automatically turn us into better people. Certainly it should and with the right help it can. Unfortunately we are all human beings and we all make mistakes all the time – some of them horrific, as I know only too well. The fact that in making them we scandalise our sceptics so that they write us off as hypocrites only adds more mistakes to the first ones! Unfortunately, with the best will in the world, being perfect is just not that easy. Actually, it's impossible!

We have all, however, been given the same debatable privilege. i.e. Free Will, and it's up to us how we use it.

Now, there's a challenge! Are we up for it?.

I am pleased to say there are two big advantages to the God option. If the basics are true, then we have help available from our counsellor, the Spirit of God. It's there for the asking. To Christians "With God all things are possible." (Matt 19:26)

The second advantage? The No-God option doesn't give us a real, lasting reason to be good apart from self-preservation, a sense of fair play and learned good manners. The God option, however, does – and it's not just the hoary old heaven/hell one either.

That reason is love. God loves us, we want to please him and love him back. What better reason could there be?

References and suggested reading

All Biblical references have been taken from the New King James version.

Suggested reading:

DAWKINS, Richard.
The God Delusion
(Transworld Publishers 2006)

McGRATH Alistair &
Joanna Collicott McGRATH
The Dawkins Delusion
(SPCK, 2007)

WARD Keith
Why there almost certainly is a God.
(Lion Hudson, 2008)

GREGORY David
Dinner with a Perfect Stranger
(Hodder & Stoughton, 2005)

FRANCES Mary
The Song of the Spinning Sun
(Trafford Publishing, 2007)

ABOUT THE AUTHOR

Mary Frances was born in 1930, youngest of seven children. She met her husband while working at Nottingham Public Libraries, and moved with him to Bristol where he became Avon County Reference Librarian. Mary herself went from 'temp secretary', legal secretary and portrait artist to running her own Art & Design company with a huge variety of other jobs in between, including election to Bristol City Council as ward representative.

In 1990 she divorced and moved to North Somerset where she took herself to college, won the prized National Senior Learner of the Year award, and spent six years as correspondent and feature writer for the local newspaper.

She now lives in Portishead and has retired from journalism to focus entirely on her first love, writing books. Her two sons live in Bristol and one of her two surviving sisters in nearby Clevedon.

Mary fully admits to 'amateur' status as philosopher and theologian, but feels that 80 years of experience, a wide and colourful job career, plus hours spent in deep thought and wide reading, qualifies her to share her conclusions with humour and common sense, without which, she says, we may as well all pack up and go home.